Things That Go Bump in the Night

"I was living on a farm in the Midwest, and ours was the only home for miles around. I remember my grandfather telling us that, since he lived many miles away from us, if he died, he would let everyone know immediately so that the family could take care of his remains.

"We were sitting in the living room of our home when we heard three loud knocks on the front door. My mother got up quickly and started for the door when she realized how isolated we were. Who could be at the door at this time of night? We all looked at the grandfather clock in the hall and saw that it was about 10:15 P.M.

"My mother got up her courage and opened the door ... to find that no one was there. No car, no truck, no horse and carriage. Nothing and no one.

"Three days later we learned that Grandpa had died in his favorite chair while reading, and Grandma saw him slump over at exactly 10:15 P.M.—the same time we heard the three loud raps on our door."

Throughout the centuries, there have been reports of rapping and knocking, invisible forces flinging water, knives, or heavy objects—even of stones falling from a cloudless sky. Some identify these occurrences as the activities of poltergeists, a term that has come to represent a wide range of bizarre experiences—from "things that go bump in the night," to inexplicable noises and sounds, to ghostly appearances of the dead.

In the chapters ahead, you will find some of the strangest stories ever told. Read them with an open mind, and you will challenge your own beliefs about the nature of the universe.

"A useful overview of the observed psychic phenomena usually referred to as hauntings, ghostly occurrences, and yes, poltergeists. The authors present all sides fairly and in a most readable fashion."

— Prof. Hans Holzer, Ph.D.
Parapsychologist and author of *Life Beyond*

Poltergeists & The Paranormal

poltergeist (pōl'ter-gīst') *n.* A ghost that manifests itself by noises and rappings. [Ger.: *poltern*, to make noises (<MHG *boldern*) + *Geist*, ghost < OHG.]

About the Authors

Dr. Philip Stander served as Chairperson of the Department of Behavioral Sciences at Kingsborough Community College from 1971 until retiring in 1995. While his published articles span a wide range of subjects, he has had a special fascination for parapsychology and the paranormal. For more than ten years he taught the course, "Principles of Parapsychology," and he continues to publish in the field. Dr. Stander also taught on the undergraduate and graduate school level at Brooklyn College, and C. W. Post College of L.I.U.

Dr. Paul Schmolling is an N.Y.U. clinical psychologist who is in private practice in New Rochelle. He is also teaching in the Mental Health Program of Kingsborough Community College, and is the co-author of Human Services in Contemporary America. He has published numerous articles on schizophrenia, drug addiction, and other subjects in abnormal psychology. In addition to his research on clinical and social issues, he has maintained a long-term interest in the paranormal. Working with Phil Stander, he has investigated several situations involving poltergeists and related phenomena.

To Write to the Authors

If you wish to contact the authors or would like more information about this book, please write to the authors in care of Llewellyn Worldwide, and we will forward your request. Both the authors and publisher appreciate hearing from you and learning of your enjoyment of this book and how it has helped you. Llewellyn Worldwide cannot guarantee that every letter written to the author can be answered, but all will be forwarded. Please write to:

Llewellyn Worldwide Ltd.

P.O. Box 64383, Dept. K682–3, St. Paul, MN 55164-0383, U.S.A.
Please enclose a self-addressed, stamped envelope for reply, or $1.00 to cover costs.
If outside U.S.A., enclose international postal reply coupon.

Poltergeists & The Paranormal

Fact Beyond Fiction

Dr. Philip Stander & Dr. Paul Schmolling

1996
Llewellyn Publications
St. Paul, Minnesota, 55164-0383, U.S.A.

FIRST EDITION
First Printing, 1996

Cover Design by Tom Grewe
Editing and Interior Design by Connie Hill

Library of Congress Cataloging-in-Publication Data
Stander, Philip, 1933–
    Poltergeists & the paranormal : fact beyond fiction / Philip
    Stander and Paul Schmolling. — 1st ed.
       p.   cm. —
    Includes bibliographical references and index.
    ISBN 1–56718–682–3 (pbk.)
    1. Poltergeists. 2. Psychokinesis. 3. Parapsychology.
  I. Schmolling, Paul. II. Title.
  BF1483.S73   1996
  133.1'4—dc20   96-36205

CIP

Llewellyn Publications
A Division of Llewellyn Worldwide, Ltd.
St. Paul, Minnesota 55164-0383, U.S.A.

Contents

Introduction

FOR MOST PEOPLE, NOTHING IS MORE TERRIFYING than having an experience that flies in the face of common sense and science. We grow up in a world of high technology, computers, television, and space science, where everything that happens has a scientific explanation or at least promises a rational, sober explanation. When we confront the unknown in the form of disembodied footsteps and voices, or the sudden appearance of someone who is known to be physically dead, we can be terribly unsettled and frightened.

One young woman told us that the sudden appearance of what she later concluded was the ghost of a former tenant horribly shocked and disturbed her. As a result of seeing this apparition of the dead, she became disoriented and confused; the very foundations of her beliefs had been shaken. She had grown up to believe that the world was an easily explainable place and that if you had the appropriate scientific tools—microscopes, telescopes, radar, sonar, scalpels, and X-rays—you could explain anything. Ghosts, poltergeists, ESP, and psychic phenomena had never been a part of her world. In school, no one had breathed a word about this strange other realm. The textbooks were devoid of a single reference to the strange and bizarre. At a party or social gathering, when a friend suggested that she'd had a vision of the future or had heard a voice whisper in her ear, the young woman was ridiculed. In her social setting, the world of psychic phenomena was equated with superstition, the occult, and the con artist.

When we began our investigation into poltergeists and psychic phenomena, we found that many reports could be dismissed as either the workings of an overactive imagination, the inability to tell the difference between a dream or fantasy and the real thing and, yes, outright blatant lies. Some of these lies are told by con artists seeking to cash in on the gullibility of those who are prepared to believe any story told, in book or movie, so long as the claim that it is "a true story" appears prominently displayed.

In September of 1977, Jay Anson's book, *The Amityville Horror,* was published as a work of non-fiction. Anson recounted the bizarre experiences of a young couple in a home they had bought in Amityville, Long Island. Their ordeal included wailing ghosts, apparitions, a demonic pig, and green slime. In March of 1978, *The New York Times* published a brief summary of an article by a reporter, Pete Stevenson, which appeared in another paper. The article contradicted significant parts of Anson's book. A police officer portrayed in the book as investigating some cloven footprints in the snow told Mr. Stevenson the incident never occurred. Another police officer mentioned in the book turned out to be nonexistent. The pastor of the local Roman Catholic Sacred Heart Church disputed the book's description of unusual occurrences involving a priest named Father Mancuso. The Psychical Research Foundation of Durham, North Carolina, held seances at the house for a television station shortly after the "haunted" couple moved out, and detected no signs of paranormal or supernatural activity.

Several films have treated poltergeists and ghost stories more humorously. While the movie, *Ghostbusters,* was designed as a humorous treatment of the subject, it used language and ideas that came directly from serious scientific literature. For example, the movie began in a college department of parapsychology where three zany scientists were devoted to investigating incidents of psychic phenomena. In reality, the first such recent effort to organize scientific "ghost hunters" and "psychic investigators" occurred in 1882 with the founding of the British Society for Psychical Research and the subsequent creation of the American Society for Psychical Research. In the 1930s the first Department of parapsychology was created at Duke University in Durham, North Carolina, by J. B. Rhine. The technique of using ESP cards with the five symbols (star, circle, square, cross, wavy lines) shown in *Ghostbusters* was actually developed under the supervision of Dr. Rhine and his wife Louisa. Controls in ESP experiments have been tightened and today are quite strict.

The movie, *Poltergeist*, fascinated us for its credible explanations and discussions of the events it depicted before all hell broke loose in a poor, besieged household. Up until the scene where the ghosts made their incredible appearances and the fiction was made even more fantastic with special effects and movie magic, discussions with the fictional parapsychologist reflected much that appeared in scientific literature. The stories that we tell in the chapters of this book were selected for their credibility and will be told without special effects, exaggeration, or undocumented embellishment.

We have gathered reports from two main sources. The first general source is professional literature including the case material of highly trained parapsychologists who have devoted themselves to the study of poltergeist phenomena. The second source is comprised of first-hand reports that we have personally gathered from witnesses we regard as reliable. These are ordinary people in the sense that they go to work, raise children, and make contributions to community life. They are not writing books or screenplays to exploit their strange experiences. They are not involved in lucrative world-wide tours to exploit and tell their strange stories of ghosts, strange lights, and voices. Instead, they are simply sharing with us their startling experiences so that others may gain understanding and thereby expand our view of a universe that may be more complicated than anyone had thought.

For example, we were provided with an anecdotal report so terrifying in its implications that we decided to devote considerable space to it in a subsequent chapter. Margo, who told us this story in all earnestness, stated that, while alone in her bedroom one night, she was suddenly attacked by some invisible force and pinned down in her bed. This experience with bizarre sexual overtones was harrowing for Margo.

Admittedly, some of the tales are terrifying. We will follow these first-hand accounts with a discussion of possible explanations. We discovered, as we attempted scientific explanations, that the events described in these stories can fit into any number of world views pictured by most of the world's philosophical, political, or religious systems of belief. It was fascinating for us to see how different people who had psychic experiences were able to explain their experiences in terms of their previously held beliefs. Very few were so shocked and traumatized that they ended by giving up their most cherished beliefs. The best example is of near death experiences (NDEs) where, during that brief period on the operating table when bodily functions seemed to stop and the person was declared to be clinically dead, the Christian reported that after leaving her body and going through the tunnel, the being of light she saw was Jesus. Buddhists reported seeing Buddha, Jewish witnesses reported seeing Moses and, in some rare and remarkable cases, some reported seeing the fires of hell.

The point is that you need to keep an open mind as you read these tales. Representatives of the scientific community—those calling themselves parapsychologists—and various religious, philosophical, and political spokespeople—will continue to offer interpretations and explanations, and we will try to be as objective, scientific, and open-minded as we have asked you to be.

CHAPTER 1

What Is a Poltergeist?

YOU WOULD THINK THAT A SIMPLE DEFINITION OF the word "poltergeist," literally translated from the German as "noisy ghost," would answer the question, "what is a poltergeist?" But the term has come to represent a wide range of strange and bizarre experiences from "things that go bump in the night," noises and sounds such as voices and footsteps, to ghostly appearances of the dead.

A poltergeist may simply appear as a disembodied voice—a voice without a visible source or body, a voice that seems to come from a distant room, over your shoulder or even inside your head. Or, it may come in the form of footsteps, or the sound of scuffling and fighting, or doors opening and shutting, or small spheres of light darting around your room, or objects such as bottles or jars which fly off a table to smash against an opposite wall, or the appearance of a long-deceased friend who returns long enough to warn you of some impending disaster.

Throughout the centuries, there have been reports of rapping and knocking, furniture moving and lifting, invisible forces flinging heavy objects, knives or water, and even of stones falling from a cloudless, clear sky, seemingly in violation of scientifically discovered natural laws. Often, the activities of the poltergeist appear to be random, senseless and mindless, as if some naughty spirit or child was being mischievous or malicious.

The poltergeist cases that appear in these chapters fall into three broad categories: *Psychokinesis, Ghosts,* and *ESP* (Extra-Sensory Perception).

Psychokinesis (PK)

The first major category, Psychokinesis (PK), often characterized as "mind over matter," continues to be studied by scientists as a living body's ability to affect or move objects or energy fields at a distance. Some theorize that PK is an energy that can leave the body and have either conscious or unconscious effects.

For example, at an electronics firm, boxes that contained delicate instruments began to mysteriously fall off shelves. After several days of this expensive breakage, the foreman noticed that the boxes fell after one of the workers passed through the storage area. In fact, he and others witnessed in amazement the boxes falling as the workman passed, and it was clear that no hand or tool was knocking them down. When the workman was transferred to another area of the plant, the phenomena ceased. The foreman, after talking to some of the company's engineers, concluded that the workman, having been engaged in a series of arguments with a co-worker, was unconsciously unleashing the energy of his anger, and the energy was pushing off the boxes as he passed. This PK explanation is often given by parapsychologists who theorize that psychokinetic energy may unconsciously leave the body of an emotionally charged person, usually an adolescent, and randomly do its damage. Such phenomena, which happen again and again, in close proximity to someone, but suddenly and unexpectedly, are classified as *Recurrent Spontaneous Psychokineses,* or RSPK.

Consider the following case: Mary, seventeen years of age, is sitting alone at home in her living room, upset that her date has stood her up. She turns on her TV set and tries to take her mind off of her disappointment. Instead, she becomes increasingly angry, even though she is trying to suppress the uncomfortable feelings of rage. Suddenly, a light bulb in the table lamp bursts and she leaps to her feet in surprise. Convincing herself that it was a freak accident, she proceeds to clean up the broken glass. Some minutes later she has returned to the sofa and TV watching, still undistracted from her anger, when the sound of smashing glass in the kitchen sends her running to see what has happened. On the kitchen floor she sees the broken pieces of a glass that has fallen from the table, but there is no one present. Mary is terrified, and her first thought is that a ghost is there in the house with her.

Can you imagine the impact on someone's psyche if such events were to happen repeatedly? Even if there are witnesses to the events, there is little comfort in the realization that all of the poltergeist activity is related somehow to your physical presence. In such cases where the poltergeist phenomena are all of a simply annoying variety involving small objects falling and breaking, parapsychologists are likely to file it under RSPK. Here the assumption is usually that the adolescent, living through a particularly troubling, crisis-laden transitional period on the way to adulthood, is emitting PK energy, sometimes in short, explosive bursts, and if an ashtray, jar, or figurine is in the way, it will go flying.

When you have read a number of the cases we present, you may choose to explain a number of them as RSPK, but if PK exists, and these cases suggest it does, then human nature as we know it will have to be redefined. If we are capable of giving off powerful bursts of PK energy in periods of great emotional stress that result in objects being moved or hurled, then there is another natural force with which we have to reckon. When you contemplate the force of PK when it is emitted unconsciously and unintentionally, then you can understand why both Russia and the U.S. Pentagon are funding research into the nature and uses of such power (a subject we will explore later, in Chapter 13).

Carl Jung and other great investigators were fascinated by the idea of poltergeists as PK phenomena. Jung introduced the terms extrovert and introvert to the general vocabulary and evolved his own school of Analytic Psychology. Most textbooks fail to note, when they describe his pioneer research in psychology, that Jung spent most of his career investigating the paranormal. To this day, Jungian analysts affirm the reality of RSPK. Some have written about a peculiar kind of poltergeist called a "luminosity," and the following is a case in point.

Betty, fifteen, is studying for her exams at her desk. The only light in her room is the small desk lamp that illuminates her textbook. From the corner of her eye she sees a light flit by.

She looks up to see what appears to be a firefly disappear behind her bed's headboard. But, as she concludes that it must have been her imagination, another pinpoint of light flies across the room from over her left shoulder and, after making a sharp right angle turn in the middle of the room, flies straight out of the window. Betty is shaken; what was a UFO, one inch in diameter, doing in her bedroom, and who would believe that she saw it? What is surprising is the great number of people who see such lights or luminosities. Even more surprising is the speculation that such poltergeists may be RSPK activity: energy from the living.

Several case studies presented in Chapter 8 involve well-documented electrical disturbances that some parapsychologists explain as RSPK. One example is the British housewife who has unintentionally destroyed thousands of dollars worth of appliances, including lighting fixtures, television sets, and telephones. It is theorized that she is an unconscious agent who somehow transmits powerful psychokinetic energy from her body. Another case discussed is that of a German office worker whose presence created havoc with the electronic equipment in her office. Some of the occurrences in her case would seem to require the actions of some intelligent, but invisible, entity—in other words, a ghost.

Ghosts

Before we consider the possibility that some poltergeists may be ghosts, the case of a consciously created poltergeist, using the collective energy of several investigators, remains one of the most fascinating on record. Until now, we have limited our discussion of poltergeists as unconsciously created PK phenomena, but the case of Philip (see Chapter 13) is unique because it represents a group effort to create a ghost out of PK energy. One summer, a group of Canadian parapsychologists gathered to explore together the possibility that some poltergeists, which act like ghosts, are projections of living energy. It has been long held by a number of researchers that some ghosts are materialized PK energy, unconsciously and unknowingly projected by the living. This particular group of parapsychologists, believing that some apparitions of loved ones, deceased and departed, are projections from the grieving living, decided to test their theory.

The Canadian researchers' experiment began with the creation of a fictional person, whom they named Philip. Philip first made his appearance in the form of rappings and tappings on a table around which members of the group sat, in the fashion of a seance. They called to Philip who, before long, began to answer questions that were addressed to him. At first, Philip's responses stuck closely to the biography the parapsychologists had created for him. Later Philip appeared to take on a life of his own.

When we recognize that there were physical effects and responses to the researchers' questions as if Philip was an independent entity, the question arises: "what is more feasible; that Philip was created by the researchers out of their living PK energy, or that this entity is a ghost, existing independently of the researchers, with a will of its own?" The second major category we will discuss is the *poltergeist as ghost,* as an actual entity independent of the living, as a so-called discarnate personality; that is, spirit without body. Keep in mind the difficulty that a working parapsychologist would have in distinguishing between a poltergeist created out of PK and one that is a ghost!

This discussion involves us in a major area of the field of parapsychology called *Survival Phenomena*. Sometimes this area of investigation is referred to as Theta Phenomena, represented by the letter of the Greek alphabet with which the word *Thanatos*, meaning death, begins. Many parapsychologists do not believe that the personality survives the death of the body. Instead, they believe that all poltergeist phenomena can be explained by at least one of the following hypotheses: (1) Fraud, and there are countless cases of these (a sample of which appears in Chapter 14), (2) Psychological illusion, hallucination, and delusion, (3) Naturalistic or Scientific explanations, (4) ESP, about which we will say more, and/or (5) Psychokinesis, consciously or unconsciously used. These skeptics do not believe in (6) Survival, or Theta, Phenomena, as many parapsychologists do, a theory which we are prepared to entertain. We will not close our minds to the survival hypothesis because we remember too well how many facts and theories were once ridiculed only to be proven true at a later time.

Consider the scientists who had "proof" that we could never use electricity to illuminate houses, or that we could never travel in space because of the inescapable force of gravity. Generally, parapsychologists rely on scientific method in exploring the unknown and in seeking answers to the world's most difficult questions. This is because scientific method has proven to be so effective in solving a great variety of human problems. There is no question that great advances have been made in such areas as astronomy, biology, physics, and space technology. To cite only one example, smallpox has been eliminated from the face of our planet because of the extraordinary effectiveness of scientific method. Aware of the successes of the hard sciences, parapsychologists have entered the laboratory with confidence and with the techniques of the new technology. One of the most difficult facts to establish, in or out of the laboratory, is the poltergeist as ghost.

Consider Margo's story, which is told in detail in Chapter 5, of an entity that entered her bedroom, pinned her down, and assaulted her. Margo's account reminds us of the legendary incubus, a raping, foul-smelling demon of mythology. Does it continue to act out its lust in modern times? Since we were the first researchers to have heard Margo's report, we were challenged to contribute our analysis and explanation. While we do this in a later chapter, we now need to complete the categorizing of poltergeist phenomena.

The following ghost story was told during night maneuvers on a military base in upstate New York. The story was told by George A. as the squad members, including one of the authors of this book, sat at the side of a road in a circle, under a starlit sky. The speaker was apparently sincere when he said he was not making anything up but was telling exactly what happened. Here is his account:

"At the time, I was living on a farm in the Midwest, and ours was the only home for miles around. When I was much younger, I remember my grandfather telling us that, since he lived many miles away from us, if he died, he would let everyone know immediately so that the family could take care of his remains. Years later, we were sitting in the living room of our home when we heard three loud knocks on the front door. My mother got up quickly and started for the door when she realized how isolated we were. Who could be at the door at this time of night? We all looked at the grandfather clock in the hall and saw that it was about 10:15 P.M. My mother got up her courage and opened the door ... to find that no one was there, no car, no truck, no horse and carriage. Nothing and no one. Then we all looked at one another and realized that Grandpa was dead. Three days later we learned that Grandpa had died in his favorite chair while reading, and Grandma saw him slump over at exactly 10:15 P.M., the time we heard the three loud raps on our door!"

When you rule out four of our six possible hypotheses, or explanations (that is, if you rule out fraud, psychological illusion, naturalistic effects, or ESP), what remains are the PK or ghost explanations. We wonder if the grandfather's ghost appeared at his family's home to knock three times on their door, thereby signaling his death, or psychokinetic energy left his body at the moment of death to signal his family. In either case, we are left with a paranormal event that begs for additional exploration and explanation. If either hypothesis is proven to be true, history will have been made and human nature will have to be redefined in our textbooks.

ESP Poltergeist

The third major category is the ESP Poltergeist, and the best illustration that we might use is the following classical tale:

"I was reading late one night while relaxing on my sofa, when I caught sight of a figure standing on the other side of the room. I was startled and sat up to face a bearded man, perhaps in his thirties, wearing a brown jacket, tan pants, and a dark green shirt open at the neck. We stared at each other for what seemed like a very long time, but could not have been more than ten seconds, when he suddenly disappeared. I have never had so strange an experience, either before or after, and cannot imagine who this person was or could have been. It remains a mystery to me."

This remains a mystery, with at least half a dozen equally viable, competing explanations. If we rule out fraud, psychological illusion, hallucination, or some naturalistic effect, we are left with the following: (1) the bearded apparition is a ghost of someone who had lived before, (2) it is an apparition of a living person whose astral self, or double, has projected itself unintentionally into someone's living room, (3) it is a man currently dwelling in a parallel dimension who has suddenly crossed over into ours, or (4) it is an ESP phenomenon.

In explaining this spontaneous appearance as possibly an ESP phenomenon, we can begin by invoking the hypothesis of *mental telepathy*. That is, the bearded image was the projection of an image in someone else's mind. The man appeared to be in the room, but was only projected into his mind.

A second ESP talent is *clairvoyance,* the ability to see that which is hidden from the senses or far away. In this case, the bearded man may have been simply envisioned as he actually appeared many miles away. Currently, the Pentagon is funding experiments at the Stanford Research Institute in clairvoyance, or *remote viewing* as they call it, and some individuals have demonstrated remarkable ability.

A third ESP talent is *precognition,* the ability to see into the future. This bearded image may be of someone who will appear in this form in the near or distant future. Some poltergeist phenomena, replete with images, noises, and things that go bump in the night, may be telepathic, clairvoyant, or precognitive images.

A final ESP talent is *retrocognition,* the ability to see into the past. The bearded apparition may be of someone who lived long ago, perhaps a former tenant, into whose past someone has accidentally tapped. General George Patton, at the height of World War II, had a vision of the sights and sounds of a battle that had been fought on a plain in North Africa more than 2,000 years ago. General Patton thought that this vision was of a battle that he had actually fought in a previous lifetime. Were the images of a past reincarnated life, or was General Patton actually seeing the past, in which he played no part, using the ESP talent of retrocognition?

In the chapters ahead we will be faced with the challenge of explaining some of the strangest stories ever told. Read them with an open mind as we explore these extraordinary tales of poltergeists.

CHAPTER 2

The Supernatural in Ancient Times

A BELIEF IN SUPERNATURAL BEINGS HAS EXISTED during all the ages, among all the peoples of the earth. To trace the origins of this belief, and to understand all of its variations throughout history, could easily occupy a team of scholars for decades. Our goal in this chapter is relatively modest: it is to sample the beliefs of the ancient peoples of the earth in regard to the supernatural. Even in this quick excursion, we will come across many accounts that uncannily foreshadow modern reports of inexplicable events.

In the Beginning

In *Passport to the Supernatural* (1972), Bernhardt Hurwood speculates that during the earliest days of human existence, *homo sapiens* were too busy coping with the environment to pay attention to things that could not be seen, heard, or touched. Once daily life was reasonably under control, and a social order was established, early people began to ponder the mysteries of nature: the movements of the sun, moon, and other heavenly bodies; the seasons of the year; and the cycles of life, death, and transformation. Gods, spirits, and ghosts were invoked to explain these and similar events. We generally agree with Hurwood, but doubt that any great length of time went by before early humans discovered supernatural entities. Every primitive society of which we know, no matter how hard the struggle for life, recognized the influence of spirits and departed ancestors. In fact, the more defenseless the people against the onslaught of natural forces, the greater the need for supernatural intervention. When confronted with drought, illness, or natural disasters such as volcanic eruptions or hurricanes, early humans summoned help from supernatural beings. Rites, incantations, and sacrifices were used to propitiate the gods, and elaborate rules were devised to protect against evil spirits and ghosts.

Early Civilizations

Most tourists who go to Egypt want to visit the great Sphinx at Giza. Along with the pyramids, it is one of the "must see" attractions in Egypt. In front of the Sphinx, a massive stone lion with the head of a man, is a stone tablet erected by Pharaoh Thutmes IV around 1450 B.C. The tablet tells a story about Thutmes as a young prince. In his wanderings, he came upon the Sphinx during the hottest time of day. He stopped to rest in the cool shadow of the monument, fell asleep, and dreamed that his father appeared to him and predicted that he

would some day inherit the throne and enjoy a long, successful reign. The voice of the dream complained of the sand that
had partly covered the Sphinx, and asked that it be removed.
When Thutmes ascended to the throne as Pharaoh, he had his
workers clear the sand from the monument, which was then
revealed in its full glory. In fact, he did have a long and fruit-
ful reign. This story has the tone of a nice fable to be told to
youngsters, but its presentation on a stone tablet suggests it
was meant to be taken literally. It contains a number of elements, including a phrophetic dream, that we will discuss further in this book.

The Semitic people of Assyria and Babylonia believed in
a full pantheon of supernatural beings long before their civilization reached its zenith of power. In *The Greatness that Was
Babylon,* H. W. F. Saggs tells us that the "ordinary man saw
himself surrounded by forces which to him were gods and devils. There was a raging demon who manifested himself in the
sand-storm sweeping in from the desert.... A host of demons
stood always ready to seize a man or a woman in particular circumstances, as, in lonely places, when eating or drinking, in
sleep, and particularly in childbirth."

The Babylonians believed in three distinct varieties of
ghosts. First were disembodied dead souls, wanderers on earth,
sometimes benign, though often not. The second type of ghost
were entities that were half human and half demon; these mon-
sters were born of couplings between humans and evil spirits.
In the Christian era, discussions were recorded between emi-
nent theologians about the consequences of sexual relations
between humans and demons known as succubi and incubi.
The third type of spirits were devils who caused whirlwinds
and afflicted humanity with plagues and pestilence.

Another recurrent theme in the history of ancient civilizations is the importance of proper burial—that is, with observation of the correct rites. People who died under conditions in which they were not buried were likely to become very unhappy spirits. This included people who were drowned, killed in battle, or murdered in some remote place. It was thought that these spirits were denied entrance to the otherworld, and, therefore, remained on earth to haunt mortals. The *ekimmu* of the Babylonians was one of these angry spirits. It was persistent and unpredictable, sometimes behaving like a poltergeist, but it could also be extremely malevolent, causing the death of the inhabitants of a house it chose to haunt.

In the ancient world, few people doubted the validity of psychical abilities such as clairvoyance, telepathy, and predicting the future. While ordinary people sometimes showed these capacities, the ability belonged, for the most part, to the seers, prophets, priests, and oracles. These special people were thought to derive their powers from the unseen world of spirits, gods, and departed ancestors. It was taken for granted that these spirits would sometimes attempt to influence the courses of events on earth. This is not to say that learned people accepted uncritically all the claims of supernatural ability that were made. In fact, the cities of the older civilization were awash with charlatans, mountebanks, and fortune tellers of all descriptions. These were met with a healthy skepticism.

Both the Old and the New Testament of the Bible provide accounts of clairvoyant dreams, apparitions, and miraculous healing. In *Exploring the Unseen World* (1959), Harold Steinhour, a research chemist with an interest in parapsychology, reminds us of a case from II Kings involving the King of

Syria, who was puzzled by the mysterious exposure of his military secrets. It seems that his enemy, the King of Israel, was fully aware of private conversations held in Syria. The advisors to the Syrian King told him that the information was provided by Elisha, the prophet, who possessed supernatural powers. Although he suspected that he might have traitors in his own camp who leaked the secrets, the Syrian King decided to take no chances; he ordered that Elisha be captured and put out of the way. It is apparent that the Syrian King, although skeptical, accepted the possibility that Elisha might be clairvoyant. In this biblical period, people found it easy to accept psychical events. Such beliefs were very much in keeping with the general atmosphere of the times.

The Bible also gives us one of the oldest ghost stories in history. It is about Saul's last night on earth. The despairing king sought out a certain woman who today would pass as a professional medium. As Shane Leslie pointed out in his *Ghost Book* (1955), even her control was described as "a familiar spirit." Saul went disguised to visit the medium at the Cave of Endor. Saul revealed to the medium that God had ceased to answer him in dreams or by word of the priests. The established clergy had failed to link him to God, and, out of desperation, he had sought the medium. The medium raised the spirit of the Prophet Samuel, Saul's ancient mentor. The dead prophet told Saul what to expect: "Tomorrow thou and thy sons will be with me." It happened that all were killed in battle on the next day.

The Ancient Greeks

The ancient Greeks deserve credit for developing the ideas of natural causation that became the foundation of modern science. However, their rational approach to the study of nature coexisted with a strong belief in all manner of supernatural events. The Greek philosopher, Phythagoras, exemplified both of these trends. He was a brilliant mathematician who was reported to conduct frequent seances at which a mystic table glided on wheels toward various signs. He interpreted the movements of this moving table as revelations from the unseen world. The device sounds very much like the modern Ouija board (trademark combining the French "oui" and the German "ja," both meaning yes). Since Pythagoras was using this kind of psychic tool in about 540 B.C., one wonders if there is really anything new under the psychical sun.

The early history of the Greeks, as told by Herodotus, is crammed with paranormal events. Herodotus, who lived between 484 and 425 B.C., set out in his early twenties to travel the known world and write its history. In his story of the great King of Lydia, Croesus, Herodotus tells about what may have been the first controlled experiment in parapsychology. Croesus received intelligence reports telling of the growing powers of his enemies, the Persians. He wondered if he ought to attack the Persians, and decided—as was the custom—to consult an oracle. However, since he was not sure of which oracle to trust, he devised a test. He sent messengers to a number of oracles in Greece and Libya. Upon the departure of his messengers, Croesus set himself to devise an action he would do that would be most impossible for anyone to guess. On the appointed day, he took a tortoise and a lamb, cut them into pieces with his own hands, and boiled them in a brass cauldron. On the same day, the hundredth day after leaving Sardis, each messenger asked the oracle what Croesus was doing at that moment—a test of their clairvoyant ability. The answers were written down and returned to Croesus.

None of the replies remain on record except that of the oracle at Delphi. The messengers to Delphi recorded that the moment they entered the sanctuary at Delphi, the Pythoness, as the priestess was called, answered in verse:

I can count the sands, and I can measure the ocean;
I have ears for the silent, and know what the dumb
    man meaneth;
Lo! on my sense there striketh the smell of the
    shell-covered tortoise;
Boiling now on a fire, with the flesh of a lamb,
    in a cauldron;
Brass is the vessel below, and brass the cover above it.

Since this was the only reply that could be considered a direct hit, Croesus was convinced of the powers of the oracle at Delphi, and proceeded to propitiate the Delphi with a magnificent sacrifice. He also sent gifts of silver and gold to the Delphic god, along with other offerings, before asking if he should go to war against the Persians. He was advised to make an alliance with the most powerful of the Greeks and to then proceed with the attacks.

The account so far reveals that a healthy skepticism existed side by side with belief in paranormal abilities. It also shows us, as Steinhour suggests, that people knew something about how to do psychical research four hundred years before the birth of Christ: "They were not all dunderheads, those prominent men of ancient times who thought there might be something in psychic stories" (*Exploring*, p. 22).

Unfortunately, the story of Croesus ends unhappily. After he was led to expect a great victory over the Persians, he went once again to the oracle at Delphi, and asked if his kingdom would be of long duration. He was told that he would be secure until "the time shall come when a mule is monarch of Media ..." Croesus was delighted with this answer since he could not imagine such a day ever coming. He grasped the meaning of the prediction too late, after he had been defeated by Cyrus, the Persian king. Cyrus was of mixed racial background; his comparison to a mule, the offspring of a horse and a donkey, was a deliberate racial slur.

The story of Croesus illustrates the importance of divination in the ancient world. In Egypt, Mesopotamia, Greece, Rome, and even Israel, it was obligatory for military and political leaders to consult an oracle before beginning any important enterprise. In subsequent chapters we will discuss the role of the medium in spiritual matters. In his book *Greek Oracles* (1965), Robert Flaceliere describes the Greek tradition of female seers. It was believed that the female spirit was best suited to intuitive, inspired divination. The earliest of these Sibyls appeared during the eighth century B.C. Their gift of divination was thought to be inspired by Apollo, who, in Greek mythology, granted the power of prophecy to his beloved, Cassandra.

The woman who served as an oracle at Delphi was chosen primarily because of her strong moral character. It appears that she fulfilled her role in an artless fashion and lacked any special knowledge. She was expected to live in a pure and chaste manner so as to be a suitable *medium* for the gods. At Delphi,

Apollo entered into her and used her vocal organs as if they were his own, very much like the "control" in modern spirit-mediumship. In some instances, the prophetess would undergo a change of voice when in a trance state, another similarity to some later accounts of modern mediums.

Clearly, the Greeks believed that their gods played an active role in the affairs of mortal men and women. They also believed that the ghost or spirits of mortals sometimes appeared on earth. One of the earliest ghost stories was originally told by Pliny the Younger. The story, retold by Catherine Crowe in *The Night-Side of Nature* (1901), concerns a house in Athens in which nobody lived because of a noisy ghost. The house, unoccupied for years, was falling to ruins when it was finally chosen by Athenodorus, the philosopher. He was aware of the reputation of the house, but accepted the challenge of living in it. Athenodorus was busy writing when the ghost first came to him. The philosopher had the presence of mind to ignore the ghost even when it began rattling its chains rather noisily. It was an old man, haggard and dirty, with dishevelled hair and a long beard. The ghost beckoned to Athenodorus to follow, but the philosopher gestured for it to wait until he finished writing. The impatient ghost came closer and shook its chains over the writer's head. Athenodorus, realizing he would not be able to work in peace, followed the ghost, who led him to a certain spot in the court which separated the two parts of the house. The apparition suddenly disappeared. After marking the spot, Athendorus arranged to have it dug up on the following day by his workers. After digging a few feet down they found the skeleton of a human being, encircled with chairs. Once the remains were reburied with appropriate ceremony, the ghost never showed itself again.

This anecdote is an early example of many to follow that involved a skeleton found on or near a haunted house. People from different backgrounds, living in various historical eras, have reported very similar ghost stories. For example, during the late 1800s many cases similar to this Athenian story were reported to the English Society for Psychical Research. At the end of this chapter, we will consider some of the reasons that have been proposed to explain the universal appearance of the spirits of the dead, but for the present, let's turn our attention to another of the great early civilizations.

The Romans

It is not surprising that Roman and Greek attitudes toward the supernatural were similar, since there was much commerce and interaction between the two cultures. Many of the Roman gods were borrowed from Greek mythology; for example, Hermes became Mercury, but retained the role of messenger to the gods. Their customs and holidays shared many common features, and there was the same respect or fear of the dead.

The Romans buried their dead in tombs and graves along-side roads leading out of their towns and cities. Tales of ghosts and vampires often centered around these roadside graves. Like the Greeks, the Romans were not concerned about the spirits of the dead who had been buried with honor. It was those who died unnatural deaths that frightened them, along with the spirits of those who had done evil deeds. Various ceremonies were performed to propitiate these spirits that were compelled to wander the earth. The ceremonies often called for the spilling of blood. In fact, the earliest gladitorial games were held in connection with important funerals.

The festival for the dead was a holiday in both Greece and Rome. During the holiday, which lasted several days, no business was carried on, temples were shut down, and everyone was uneasily aware of the spirits among the living. The doors of the houses were smeared with pitch and the citizens chewed whitehorn to keep the spirits away. In Rome, Lemuria or Lemuralia, as the holiday was called, took place in May and called for a special ritual performed by heads of households. Late at night, this person would walk barefoot through the house, making the sign of the horns with the thumb crossed over the two middle fingers and the forefinger and little finger extended. While going through the house, the homeowner would throw beans over his shoulder and recite incantations—nine times—without looking around. Presumably the spirits followed and picked up the beans. With a clash of brass cymbals, the gathered spirits were ordered from the premises. That this festival was a recognized holiday tells us a great deal about the active roles played by the departed in ancient Rome. Our Halloween has its origins in this pagan holiday.

The distinguished French scientist, Camille Flammarion, reminds us in *Haunted Houses* (1924) of a story told by Cicero, the famous Roman orator. Cicero told of two friends who arrived in a certain town and went to separate lodgings. During the night, one of the men was awakened by an apparition of his friend who asked him to come to his aid immediately. The first traveler assumed that he had been dreaming and went back to sleep. The apparition appeared again and again, but was each time ignored by the tired traveler. When the apparition appeared for the last time, it was bleeding and disfigured. The ghost told him that it was now too late to save him since he had been murdered by his host. The ghost now pleaded to be avenged, telling his companion to go to the gate of the town at sunrise, where he would find a cart filled with dung. The ghost predicted that his body would be found hidden in the middle of the cart. The friend obeyed these instructions, found the body just as predicted, and arrested the driver. He made arrangements for the body to be buried with customary rites and honors so that his friend could rest in peace. Cicero took this story as evidence of divine intervention in the affairs of men, although no gods actually appeared in the account.

Cicero's writings seem to contradict themselves in regard to the supernatural. On the one hand, he told ghost stories involving dream divination, but he also presented himself as a skeptic. In his famous essay "On Divination," Cicero attacked the dream interpreters, astrologers, and diviners who were apparently quite numerous in Rome. In fact, he was one of the first to present an argument that has been raised many times since by doubters of paranormal phenomena. "And in the infinite series of ages," wrote Cicero, "chance has produced many more extraordinary results in every kind of thing than it has in dreams; nor can anything be more uncertain than conjectural interpretation of diviners which admits not only of several, but often of absolutely contrary sense ... superstition ... has oppressed the intellectual energies of all men, and betrayed them into endless imbecilities."

As M. Ullmann and S. Krippner suggest in their book, *Dream Telepathy* (1973), Cicero's complaint was doubtless a minority voice in a world where superstition was a way of life. It was only in recent times that parapsychologists have found ways to take into account the operation of chance and coincidence. We will describe some of those methods in Chapter 13.

Chapter 3

Early European Cases

THE WORD *POLTERGEIST* CAN BE TRACED TO GER-
man folklore, and refers to a native spirit, imp, or goblin, with
some unpleasant characteristics. In his book *Poltergeist: Tales
of the Supernatural* (1993), Harry Price declared that while the
ordinary ghost of storybooks is usually quiet, noiseless, and
benevolent, the poltergeist is mischievous, destructive, noisy,
cruel, erratic, thievish, ruthless and vampiric. A ghost *haunts,*
he stated, but the poltergeist *infests*. Price further informed us
that the term is a compound of the German verb *polter*, to make
noise by knocking, rattling, or tumbling things about, and the
noun, *geist*, or ghost. It is related to *polterzimmer*, a room set
aside for children where they can make noise and smash their
toys. Another related term is *polterabend*, the night before a
wedding, when it was customary in parts of Germany to make
noise and smash things outside the girl's house.

Martin Luther (1483–1546) was one of the first to use the term, ascribing such goings-on to the devil. However, poltergeist outbreaks were reported throughout European history, long before the word became part of the language. The village of Bingen-am-Rhein was the scene of two such outbreaks in 355 and 856. The standard tricks were reported, including stone-throwing, rapping, and people being dumped out of bed. Also reported was a mysterious voice that revealed embarrassing secrets of the villagers.

Herbert Thurston, in *Ghosts and Poltergeists* (1954), provided examples of early cases, some drawn from monastic records. In 530, St. Cyprian recounted how the physician to King Theodoric endured flights of stones within his house. As might be expected, this activity was suspected of being the work of the devil. In the twelfth century, Gerald of Wales described how he had come across two houses in South Pembroke where "foul spirits" threw lumps of dirt, as if to express contempt for the occupants. In one of the houses the spirit damaged clothing, no matter how carefully it was locked away. In the other house, the spirit mocked the occupants and revealed their guilty secrets. Gerald reported that rites of exorcism failed to stop these events; in fact, the priests themselves were subjected to the same kind of insults as the townspeople. He concluded that sacraments were effective only against true demons, but not against mischievous nature spirits.

A distinction between relatively harmless spirits and more violent ones was made fifty years later by William of Auvergne, Bishop of Paris. He spoke of a particularly nasty kind of demon that attacked the holy persons living in monasteries. He cited the example of St. Christine of Sommeln, who was viciously assaulted by invisible entities:

they banged her head against the wall, slashed her, and threw filth at her.

In *The Encyclopedia of Witchcraft and Demonology,* Russell Robbins (1950) tells of a 1460 case of unexplained mischievous events in Spain, and of another naughty poltergeist who played tricks on a young servant girl in Bologna in 1579. Ten years later, Peter Binsfeld, a bishop and major German authority on the treatment of witches, justified a tenant's breaking a lease if his house was troubled by noisy demons.

An early case that included considerable detail was presented by Adrian De Montalembert, confessor to Francis I of France. Published at Paris in 1528, it told the "wonderful history" of the spirit that troubled the Nuns of Saint Peter at Lyons. It was unearthed by Andrew Lang, who made the story available to English readers in *Cock Lane and Common Sense* (1894). According to Lang, the original version had "an agreeable air of good faith."

The nuns at the abbey enjoyed a somewhat undisciplined lifestyle prior to 1516, after which stricter rules were put into place and things tightened up. Prior to the reform, the nuns had been coming and going as they desired. One of the members of the order, Sister Alis De Telieux, succumbed to the temptations presented by the relaxed atmosphere. As sacristan, it was her duty to take care of relics and sacred objects. One day, she departed for the city taking with her some of the valuables belonging to the community. About eight years later, in 1524, Alis died, abandoned by all, in the fields of a little village. She died in disgrace without prayers or proper burial. Shortly after her death, a number of bizarre events were reported.

The medium or agent of the strange events that began in 1526 was Sister Antoinette, aged eighteen. One night, as she lay half asleep in bed, alone in her room, someone lifted her veil, made the sign of the cross on her forehead, and kissed her tenderly. She was surprised but not frightened by this experience. Since no one else appeared to be in her room, she assumed that she had been dreaming. A few days later, she began to hear rapping noises under her feet. The sounds followed her everywhere and even seemed to intensify during worship. The sounds were only heard when she was present. The historian of these events, de Montalembert, testified that he heard these sounds, and, at his request, as many raps would be made as he desired.

Antoinette told the astonished nuns that she had often dreamed of Alis, the former sacristan. Perhaps the sounds were being made by the spirit of Alis. This supposition was apparently confirmed by appropriate raps when the entity was asked to identify itself. When the spirit was asked if it wished to be buried in the abbey, it answered strongly in the positive. This led to a search for Alis' body which was found, disinterred, and returned to the abbey. The rapping noises became more and more frantic as the body was brought closer to the abbey. Elaborate services were conducted to save the soul of the nun who had broken her vows by stealing sacred relics from the abbey. Antoinette acted as medium for the departed sister; she went so far as to kneel at the feet of the Abbess and beg for mercy, saying "have mercy on me," as though she were Alis. The appeal was so moving that the bishop, who was in attendance, granted absolution.

The raps became fainter from that time on. Antoinette received a communication from Alis that her penance in purgatory had been reduced from thirty-three years to thirty-three days. (It was suspected by some Protestants that this story was cooked up to embarrass them, since they did not believe in Purgatory.) In any case, it was during this period that Antoinette experienced a levitation accompanied by intense rapping.

The drama was approaching its final act, which took place on the feast of St. Benedict, patron saint of the order. The nuns were seated at their table, and a reading was in progress, when thirty-three powerful blows were struck by some invisible hand again signifying the reduction in Alis' penance. Alan Gauld and A. D. Cornell, in their book *Poltergeists* (1979), identify this case as a precursor to later cases in which communication has been made with a purported spirit by means of raps. Such cases, they go on, are surprisingly numerous, and it is through one of them, at Hydesville in 1848, that the Spiritualist movement began (a case we will discuss in Chapter 6). Gauld and Cornell add that cases involving raps as communication are still being reported in recent times, and they give several examples of these.

It was not until the 1800s that serious investigators began to supply lengthy, written accounts of cases involving paranormal events. The case that follows is one of the most influential and best-known of the early nineteenth century.

The Seeress of Prevorst

This case, reported by a German physician named Justinus Kerner, deals with the mysterious illness of a woman with psychic abilities. Dr. Kerner's account first appeared in book form in 1829 and became a best seller of the period, going into numerous editions and was translated into English by Catherine Crowe in 1845 (*The Seeress of Prevorst*). The title page begins, "The Seeress of Prevorst, Being Revelations Concerning The Inner-Life of Man, and the Inter-Diffusion of a World of Spirits in the One we Inhabit." As the title suggests, it is not primarily a poltergeist case. We include it because poltergeist events were reported in the presence of the central figure. The case is one of those in which poltergeist phenomena appear in the midst of a wide range of paranormal events. As will become obvious to the reader, poltergeist events are intertwined with other unusual events that typify a certain historical period. This case belongs to the period when mesmerism, magnetic healing, and hypnosis preoccupied the medical profession.

Dr. Kerner, the chief physician in the city of Weinsberg, practiced medicine throughout his adult life, but was also a well-known poet and writer. According to Eleanor T. Smith, author of *Psychic People* (1968), the townspeople of Weinsberg so revered the doctor that they gave him a house at the foot of Schloss Weibertreu, where he extended hospitality to people from all walks of life. One of those who came to his home in 1826 seeking help was Friederika Hauffe. It was immediately obvious that she was seriously ill. She had lost all her teeth, appeared wasted away, and was unable to rise without help. If she did not receive a spoonful of broth every few minutes she would faint or go into spasms. The doctor wrote that she "had many frightful symptoms, and fell into a trance every evening at seven o'clock. This used to begin with crossing her arms, and prayer." Then she would stretch out her arms and begin to talk with her eyes shut, and her face "lighted up."

The patient, who was referred by her relatives, had been ill since her marriage in 1819. Dr. Kerner was sought because he had written about Mesmer's theory of animal magnetism. Friederika came from the village of Prevorst, whose people were well known for their belief in tales of the supernatural.

As a child, Friederika claimed that she saw and conversed with ghosts, as did her sister. When her parents announced her engagement to a cousin, Friederika became acutely depressed. This mood was deepened when, on her wedding day, she attended the funeral of her minister, an elderly man to whom she was devoted. From that day forward, she suffered fevers, spasms, and various mysterious ailments. After being given homeopathic remedies over a period of several years, her health improved and she was able to give birth to two children. However, the first one died within a few months and the second had to be cared for by relatives.

Friederika soon became the apparent focal point of a variety of poltergeist-type events. Various objects were observed by witnesses to rise up and move about her room. There were noises such as loud knocking, hammering, the throwing of sand, and the rustling of paper that she interpreted as some of the ways that spirits attract attention to themselves.

Once Dr. Kerner entered a room where she was asleep in bed, fully dressed down to her boots, "which were fastened on her feet by hooks." As he watched, "the boots were taken off her feet by an unseen hand—carried through the air to where her sister was standing by the window—and set down beside her. Mrs. Hauffe lay perfectly still the whole time, and knew nothing of it when I awoke her; her sister wept, and did not like to touch the boots again." Kerner added the following testimony to his book: "I can bear witness, not only to the sounds of throwing, knocking, etc., but a small table was flung into a room without any visible means; the pewter plates in the kitchen were hurled about, in the hearing of the whole house—circumstances laughable to others, and which would be so to me, had I not witnessed them in my sound mind."

One of her most impressive psychic feats centered on a spirit, a man with a squint, who began to disturb her sleep. The doctor recognized this man from her description. He had died some years ago while under suspicion that he had arranged a crooked financial deal for which another man had been blamed. Mrs. Hauffe received the idea that the spirit was worried about a certain document which had not been discovered after his death. The spirit told her it was on a desk in a certain room. Her description was so precise that Kerner recognized the office as belonging to Judge Heyd. When Kerner told him of his patient's vision, the judge was astounded, since he had been sitting in the very position described by Mrs. Hauffe on that day. The missing document was found, thanks in part to Mrs. Hauffe's accurate statement that the document was not in correct numerical order and that it would have a bend in the corner. The document showed that the accused man was innocent of any wrongdoing.

The patient reported similar encounters with spirits that wanted to be absolved of crimes they had committed while on earth. One of these was the spirit of a man named Belon, who had defrauded orphans in his official capacity as Guardian of Orphans. At Kerner's request, the mayor of Weinsberg examined the town records, and found that a man of that name died in 1740. Further examination of the records confirmed the likelihood that he was indeed guilty of the irregularities to which he had confessed to Mrs. Hauffe.

The sensational success of Kerner's book, *The Seeress of Prevorst,* was not due entirely to the amazing events it described but to its spiritual content. In her trance state, Mrs. Hauffe taught that each human being is composed of body, spirit, and soul which are enveloped in a sheath called the *Nervengeist.* When the person dies, this Nervengeist decays and disintegrates. It is this sheath that makes earthbound spirits visible to the living, and that is responsible for the "inter-diffusion" of spirits in the everyday world. Mrs. Hauffe also believed that with the passage of time, the soul passes through visible circles or spheres indicating depths of goodness.

In a system reminiscent of the Kabbala of Jewish mystics, Mrs. Hauffe preached that numbers were attached to these spheres. One number represented the inner life while another represented the human being in relation to the world, and so on. In her trance state, she spoke in a strange language, derived from ancient times, with elements of Coptic, Hebrew, and Arabic. She also related numbers to words in a mystical way. With her number system, she predicted the hour and day of her death. Although Kerner doubted her number system, he admitted that her prediction proved to be accurate. In fact, Friederika Hauffe died in 1829 at the age of twenty-eight, having been enfeebled by the strain of mediumship.

After her passing, a circle of mystics was formed to study Mrs. Hauffe's revelations. At the fringe of this mystical group was C. Adam von Eschenmayer, a philosopher and disciple of Immanuel Kant, who personally investigated the case. The group members considered Mrs. Hauffe's teachings related to those of Plato and Pythagoras, as well as to those of current spiritualists. For several years, they published a journal devoted to mystical speculations.

According to Colin Wilson (*The Mammoth Book of the Supernatural*, 1991), Kerner's book was no longer taken seriously during the second half of the nineteenth century when scientific reaction against spiritualism increased. Kerner was criticized for taking Hauffe's claims seriously. "When the seeress was alive," Kerner responded, "... did any of those who now write volumes of refutation ever take the trouble to … examine her for themselves? No: they sat still at their desks, and yet considered themselves better able to pronounce on these facts than the calm, earnest and profound psychologist, Eschenmayer, who examined everything on the spot, and in person …."

The historical importance of Kerner's book on the seeress, according to Frank Podmore, was that it laid the foundation for the movement of modern spiritualism. Without any evidential basis, Podmore believed that Mrs. Hauffe resorted to trickery to satisfy her vanity; yet, she was possessed of true religious impulse.

Colin Wilson regarded this case as "a thoroughly typical case of poltergeist phenomena caused by a medium." If the poltergeist events themselves were unspectacular compared to other famous cases, Wilson suggested, it was because Friederika was weak from the moment Kerner first met her. The spirits manifested themselves by using her energy, eventually draining her completely.

The next case, which also involves a young woman with extraordinary abilities, anticipates the modern cases involving electrical phenomena that comprise Chapter 8.

Angelique Cottin, the Electric Girl

Angelique, a fourteen-year-old girl of La Perriere, France, first demonstrated her powers on January 15, 1846. While at work with other girls in a shop, she was startled when the glove-making frame at which she was seated began to jump about. The heavy oak table on which the frame rested began to make strange movements. Furniture began to back away from her as though repelled by some magnetic force. It was difficult for Angelique to sit down, since the chair would run from her. Even when others held the chair down, it persisted in moving away from her. Feathers and other objects would apparently react to her, sometimes by moving toward her, sometimes away from her.

Although the witchcraft era was clearly over, some thought she was possessed and in need of exorcism. However, a scientific attitude prevailed and Angelique was turned over to M. de Faremont, a local landowner who carefully studied and documented the inexplicable events around the girl. He became convinced that deception could not explain her performances. For example, he observed a heavy bin lift off the ground at her approach. The only point of contact between the object and Angelique was a billowing out of her petticoat. The bin, according to Faremont, was instantly lifted to a height of three or four inches above the ground and continued to rise and fall several times a minute. He explained the events by suggesting that she had somehow acquired an electrical charge that was being discharged in somewhat unpredictable fashion. She was able to give violent electric shocks to other people.

Colin Wilson speculated about the nature of the current that emanated from the girl. Although she was able to lift a heavy tub with a man sitting in it, she was not able to influence purely metallic objects. When she was tired, the current would be lessened in power. The current was most powerful when she was standing on bare earth and was decreased if she was on a carpet. During the several months when the phenomena were most intense, she slept on a cork mat. It seemed possible then that the current was not the standard form of electricity but a biological force that she acquired from the earth.

Angelique was next put on exhibition in a nearby town by her parents who seized the opportunity to earn some extra money. There was some concern about the movements of her dress. However, a local doctor investigated and satisfied himself that the dress did not conceal a contraption of some sort. It strains credibility to believe that this girl, described as dull and of small stature, would at the age of fourteen suddenly acquire the skills of a professional conjuror. Numerous respectable people were convinced that she had no confederates, or special equipment, and that the effects were genuine.

Angelique was sent to Paris to be investigated by a number of scientists including Francois Arago, the famous astronomer and physicist who was known as a free thinker and determined materialist. The same performances observed by so many before were repeated for Arago and his colleagues. Again, tables and chairs moved away from her and a chair was flung against a wall even though it was being held by the investigator. It was observed that pieces of paper were attracted to her, and that pith balls suspended by thread were set in motion by her.

The research ended in a decided anticlimax. A formal committee was established by the Academy of Science to continue the investigations. Various measuring instruments were set up to determine what kind of current was involved but the tests were unproductive. After several days of no results, the tests were abandoned. Angelique was sent home, and never again demonstrated the phenomena that made her briefly famous.

Catherine Crowe, who reported the case of Angelique Cottin in *The Night Side of Nature*, suggested that poltergeist phenomena may be electrical in nature. She described another woman, Mlle. Emmerich, who was able to give people electric shocks, not only on contact, but also from a distance. She had acquired the power after an accident in which she had received a severe fright.

Catherine Crowe also reported instances in which people under hypnosis became capable of administering electric shocks to others. In addition, she had met one person who claimed to be able to do it at will. If certain people are able to produce strong electric currents, it would help to explain at least some of the events that occur in poltergeist outbreaks.

Such poltergeist cases involving electromagnetic phenomena persist to this day. The story of the Russian peasant woman (described in Chapter 13), reported in Sheila Ostrander and Lynn Schroeder's *Psychic Discoveries Behind the Iron Curtain* (1970) is typical. In the 1960s, when Russian parapsychologists were convinced that some poltergeist activity was the result of electromagnetic energy radiating out of living bodies, Kulagina was brought into a laboratory to be tested, investigated, and filmed. Under the most strict and rigorous of testing conditions to assure that there was no fraud or trickery—no hidden magnets, strings, stage magic, or confederates—Kulagina was observed using mind energy to move matchsticks and assorted objects across a table. Among the fifteen scientists invited to observe was Dr. Glen Boles, an American psychiatrist, who attested to Kulagina's ability. As in the cases reported in this chapter, after performing Kulagina appeared drained of energy, the electroencephalograph to which she was hooked up showing over fifty times the normal electrical output from her brain and nervous system. Ostrander reported that, after such sessions, Kulagina would sleep for some two or three days, seemingly "recharging her battery," as one observer put it.

In an interview with the American psychic, Donna D'Alessandro, the hypothesis was suggested that some individuals attract disembodied spirits or invisible entities whose energy, combined with that of the living subject, produce a wide range of poltergeist activity, including electromagnetic phenomena and the hurling of objects and rocks.

We conclude this chapter with a case involving one of the most typical tricks in the poltergeist repertoire—rock throwing. As we have seen, flying rocks and stones have been reported in the earliest poltergeist infestations—and continue to be reported.

The Paris Poltergeist

As related by Brian Inglis in *Natural and Supernatural: A History of the Paranormal* (1992), the Paris poltergeist of 1849 meets the standards of an evidential case. In fact, the case was described in detail by the official publication of the French police. When workers started to open up a new street between the Sorbonne and the Pantheon, a little house that stood nearby suddenly became the center of attention. Every evening it was assailed by a hail of projectiles as if under siege. The projectiles were mostly paving stones; some were fragments of the nearby demolished walls but others were entire stones of such weight that no human could have thrown them so far. "In vain has a surveillance been exercised," complained the official report, "day and night, under the personal direction of the Commissary of Police, and able assistants." The Head of Security was continually on the spot, and watchdogs were let loose in the adjoining enclosures, but no one was able to explain the phenomena. The projectiles, which continued to rain down on the house, seemed to be launched from a great height above the heads of observers who stationed themselves on the roofs of surrounding houses. The rocks seemed to come from a great distance, reaching their aim with mathematical precision and without deviating from the trajectory evidently designed for them. Although the author of the report deplored the tendency of the public to ascribe the phenomena to other-worldly means, he admitted that the police observers were at a complete loss to otherwise explain them.

CHAPTER 4

Poltergeists on the Attack

ANECDOTAL ACCOUNTS OF INCUBI AND SUCCUBI attacking innocents in their beds abounded during Medieval times, but belief in the incubus and succubus spirits precedes the Middle Ages and can be traced back to ancient cultures. The incubus was thought to be a male demon who lay on sleeping women in order to have sexual intercourse with them and otherwise abuse them. The succubus was described by theologians and scholars to be a female demon who sought to have intercourse with sleeping men.

While various cultures gave these demons different names, they all had in common their sexually insatiable appetites and their habit of assaulting humans as they slept at night. The ancient Hebrews had depicted Lilith as a Hebrew queen and mother of all succubi, the Assyrians wrote of the female demon Lili, the Arabs had the Jinn, the ancient Greeks and Romans saw nymphs haunting their woods, the Greeks described predatory sirens, the Celts were tormented by the Dusii and the Hindu by the Bhut. These female demons of ancient civilizations made such sustained and unquenchable sexual demands that the encounters would sometimes prove fatal for the male. In most instances, the encounters with suc- cubi would end in psychological turmoil or physical harm.

Medieval Beliefs

During the Middle Ages, belief in the incubi/succubi phenom- ena reached a fevered pitch. So powerful were these manifes- tations that Christian demonologists came to believe that these spirits or entities could resist the rites of exorcism. While some Christian authorities were skeptical of their existence, St. Augustine was convinced that they existed and that it was "sheer impudence" to deny their existence.

The ability of these demons to take human form was a source of human terror. At times, the demon would appear as a familiar person, often taking the form of an enemy; at other times, the form would be that of the poor victim's husband or wife, friend or lover.

When the Bishop Silvanus was accused of sexually assaulting a nun, he swore that an incubus was guilty by taking possession of his form. A number of nuns, at various times during this Medieval period of frenzy and hysteria, claimed that they had actually slept with Christ. While the nuns had been taught that they in fact were the "wives of Christ," this union was interpreted by Christian theologians to constitute a *spiritual* union; to have claimed otherwise, as did the nuns, was considered blasphemous.

When children were born to these nuns, the belief was that the incubi had impregnated them. First, a demon in the form of a succubus would have intercourse with a human male and gather his semen. Then taking the form of an incubus, it would inseminate a human female. Bishop Silvanus (as cited by Summers, 1989) recorded the following: "The learned William of Paris, Confessor of Philip Le Bel, lays down: that there exists such beings as are commonly called the incubi or succubi and that they indulge their burning lusts, and that children, as it is freely acknowledged, can be born from them, is attested by the unimpeachable and unshaken witness of many men and women who have been filled with foul imaginings by them, and endured their lecherous assault and lewdness."

The nature of the sexual potency of demons was debated. St. Thomas Aquinas believed that in its spirit form the demon was sterile and incapable of producing semen, but when the demon dreamt, it could as a result of a wet dream produce semen, and then when having intercourse with a human female impregnate her with this semen. Thus, St. Thomas Aquinas entertained the paradox—the seeming contradiction—of the demon being both virgin and father.

The increasing number of reports of humans being attacked and having relations with evil spirits led Pope Innocent VII to proclaim in a Papal Bull that this was a consequence of the failure of faith. The Pope reasoned that men and women were more and more susceptible to assaults by incubi and succubi because they were forgetting their faith. On the question of whether children could result from such unions between demons and humans, the Pope declined to decide.

As proof of demon attacks, victims would often show bruises and wounds, some of which were on the back and places seemingly inaccessible to the hands of the victim. Children born of these unions also appeared to have been harmed, deformed, or were odd in some other physical way. As the hysteria spread, even twins came to be suspected of having been spawned by an incubus. When Martin Luther emerged on the scene to lay the basis for the Protestant faith, he was accused of heresy for his rebellion against the Catholic Church. The eighteenth-century Franciscan theologian, Ludovico Maria Sinistrari, attempting to account for Luther's attacks upon the Church, stated that a demon incubus had to have donated his seed to create "that damnable heresiarch Martin Luther." In his lifetime, Luther never rejected the Medieval belief in the incubus, insisting that any odd-looking child must be a product of demons and consequently should be killed at birth.

Whether or not a sexual assault by demons led to conception, and regardless of the fact that the bruises and wounds and destructive poltergeist activity associated with such attacks was submitted as evidence that the sexual attack was against the will and wishes of the victim, any relation with an incubus and succubus was deemed to be a sin. Therefore, anyone suspected of having been to bed with a demon was punished for diabolism and sexual perversion.

The claim that demons were responsible became increasingly common. Under torture, some would "confess" to having been raped by an incubus. Conveniently, the claim became an excuse to accuse an adulterous spouse of laying with a demon. Unmarried mothers with children born to them out of wedlock were accused of relations with an incubus as a way out of marriage. Such claims continued to be made through time. In the seventeenth century, a noblewoman gave birth to a child during her husband's four-year absence. When she claimed that she had been duped by an incubus who took her husband's form while he was away and impregnated her, no one publicly doubted the lady's honor.

When the demons came as night visitors, they came in the flesh, but they reportedly appeared in dreams, as well. When a devout churchman or religious person had an erotic dream, the assumption was that this must be the work of the Devil, for no moral, religious person could willfully create such dreams.

D. H. Rawcliffe (*Occult & Supernatural Phenomena* (1952) offered another view of these reports of demonic attacks. "The ecstatic experiences of many individuals have consisted of euphoric hallucinations in which scenes of brutal sadism and perverse sexual orgies predominate; here may be most clearly seen the common relationship between euphoric experiences and sexual disturbances." This is Rawcliffe's interpretation that the Devil, or demons, may not have been responsible. According to this view, sexual repression caused by great guilt induced during the Medieval period produced erotic dreams or hallucinations in which the incubi and succubi appeared. Unable to admit their strong sexual feelings, denying and repressing them, when these feelings were manifest in dreams, the interpretation was that the Devil or demons were tormenting them. It is interesting to note that *incubo* is Latin for nightmare and *incubare* means to lie upon. Whatever the interpretation, these reports continued through history.

Colonial American Witchcraft

With the great transplantation from Europe to the colonies of America, belief in entities that could attack an innocent was carried over. In seventeenth-century New England, poltergeist phenomena and possessions were almost always blamed on a woman who was subsequently accused of being a witch. In an early case, Samuel Parris, a Puritan minister of Salem Village, witnessed bizarre events and behavior associated with his daughter and a niece. He came to believe that they were possessed by the Devil because of their association with his housekeeper, Tituba. Tituba was accused of being a witch, and rumors of witchcraft spread, resulting in trials and executions.

The belief was that witches were in league with the Devil and sometimes possessed by him. Witches would perform the rituals of "maleficium" in order to do harm to others by supernatural means. As Carol F. Karlsen noted, "Witches would enter men's bed chambers at night and prevent them from sleeping by beating, choking, biting, sitting on, lying on, and smothering them" (*The Devil in the Shape of a Woman*, 1984). The Puritans of Salem believed that the greatest of all sins was that of sexual seduction, which drew others into the sin to make great numbers of people equally guilty of the sin.

The challenge of the village elders of Salem was to identify the witches who were to blame. Since the women suspected of causing the poltergeist phenomena: chaos, physical harm and possession, would deny their guilt when accused, confessions were extracted by torture. When a form of torture called the dunking chair was used to determine whether a woman was a witch, the poor accused was doomed in a nightmarish catch-22. She was judged to be innocent when submerged in a lake or pond while strapped in the dunking chair if her drowned body floated to the surface, and guilty if her drowned body remained at the lake's bottom.

An alternative theory of who these condemned women were has emerged. Some believe that the accused were mid-wives or village healers whose theories about nature and ill-ness were at odds with the religious and medical establishment of the time. Another view was that greed for the property of the accused contributed to the psychological hysteria that spread. According to the latter view, some of the elders encouraged the charges made in order to acquire the property of the executed women. When the hysteria passed, and trade began to preoccupy the concerns of the villagers, the witch hunting came to an end, as did the reports of levitating girls, flying brooms, and breaking dishes.

The Case of the Schiel Family

In 1581 at Tottelstedt, Germany, the family of Hans Schiel, his wife Margareta, and sons Hans and Martin lived in a small peasant cottage. The case of the Schiel family was document-ed by a priest, Johann Korner, whose story begins one night as the family lay down to rest. Suddenly, the peace of the night was broken by lumps of earth striking them and all parts of the cottage. They were frightened and mystified because they could not understand where it was coming from. The next day, they made no mention of the brief period of terror during the previous night to visiting neighbors and relatives, but once inside the cottage, the visitors were struck with lumps of dirt. As Cornell relates the story (*Poltergeists*, 1979), when one of the Schiel brothers brought in a fist-sized piece of clay that had hit the cottage and laid it on the floor, teeth marks suddenly appeared in the clay as if it was being bitten by some invisible entity.

On another occasion, stones fell upon them and one landed (in the words of the family) on the toe of a "disbeliever," causing him great pain. Members of the family continued to experience pain as parts of their bodies became swollen from the pelting; the poltergeist attacks increased.

When he could bear no more, Schiel went to the local priest for help. Upon hearing of the attacks, the priest at first refused to come, insisting that the family's house be destroyed piece by piece, in order to rid it of the evil presence. Responding to Schiel's insistent pleading, the priest agreed to help, but as soon as he entered the house, he was immediately pelted with dirt. The priest said mass and, for a short period of time, all was quiet. Then, without any prior warning, the violence returned with a fury. In desperation, the Schiels sought help from high government officials, who examined and methodically investigated the house and events, but to no avail; their conclusion was, "that the phenomena were the work of Satan rather than of wicked men or magicians."

The poltergeist attacks continued with even greater fury; the elder son was almost strangled and an axe flying through the air barely missed the father's head. Again, Schiel sought help and, this time, two priests and their helper prayed for days in an effort to rid the house of the evil demons. Some period of peace did follow, and when the disturbances returned, the activities were much weaker. The Suffrogan Bishop, himself, came to the house, flung himself on the floor face down, and prayed in full robes. As Cornell concludes,

"From that day and hour onwards the Devil was heard no more in the town of Tottlestadt."

Since in most cases of reported poltergeist phenomena the disturbing activities tend to die away in a matter of weeks, it continues to be debated whether the Bishop "cured" the house, or if it was simply time for the attacks to stop, or if the energy had been used up and dissipated from whatever the source. Once again, we see the presence of young adolescents in the Schiel home, and the question is raised about whether the energy released to attack family members, relatives, and neighbors derived from the repressed, pent-up sexual drives of the pubescent boy, but, in this case, a number of the attacks occurred when the boys were out of the room or away from home. Whether these sadistic attacks were sexually motivated remains an unanswered question.

The Case of Eleanore Zugun

Leaping into the twentieth century, we find the 1926 case of a Rumanian girl, Eleanore Zugun, who believed that her invisible attacker was "Dracu," the Devil. The story began when Eleanore found some money and bought candy with it. Her grandmother, then 105 years old, whom Eleanore called a "witch," told her that this candy that she had eaten contained the Devil and that she would never be free from him. Soon after, objects began to mysteriously move and float in her presence. Two eyewitnesses, a priest named Macarescu and a schoolmaster named Teodorescu, described objects rising and flying toward them. When the priest could do nothing to stop the poltergeist attacks, Eleanore was taken from her home and placed in an insane asylum.

German parapsychologist Fritz Grunewald read about the eyewitness accounts in a local newspaper, and decided to intervene. Along with Kubi Klein, a journalist, and Victor Setnick, the owner of a busline near Talpa, Grunewald managed to get Eleanore released from the asylum. As Cornell describes it in his treatment of the case, Grunewald brought her to the monastery of Gorovei and documented the case; "Grunewald's notes, published after her death, are the fullest minute-by-minute record of poltergeist phenomena prior to the invention of the tape recorder."

Grunewald's account began with an assault on Eleanore's body by an invisible entity; in his presence she was repeatedly subjected to bites and welts which appeared on her hands and wrists. When he raised the sleeve of her blouse, he saw that these marks, along with scratches and heavy welts, had been caused to appear on her covered arm. On another occasion, when Eleanor raised a cup of tea, Grunewald could see a bite mark with both rows of teeth impressions appearing on her wrist.

Captain Seton-Karr relates this eyewitness account: "I was present on 5 October when the so-called 'stigmatic' markings appeared on the face, arms and forehead of Eleanore Zugun under conditions which absolutely precluded the possibility of Eleanore producing them by scratching or other normal means. The marks were photographed in my presence."

On May 15, 1926, Grunewald observed nineteen separate phenomena, including objects from the kitchen cupboard being thrown about, just missing Eleanore, and coins falling from above her head. To Grunewald, it seemed impossible for her to have thrown these since both her hands were on the table throughout the activity. His plan was to move Eleanore to Berlin so that he could observe her in his laboratory and closely observe the poltergeist activity, but before he could follow through, he had a massive heart attack and died at the age of forty-one.

Eleanore's family had treated her very badly over the years and she was not happy to be returned to them. After spending a short time with her family, Eleanore was rescued by the Viennese Countess Zoe Wassilko-Serecki. The Countess had a long-standing interest in psychical research and had read about the strange events surrounding Eleanore. After arranging to have Eleanore live with her and seeing how well the girl adjusted to her new surroundings, the Countess witnessed strange phenomena. To determine whether some physical abnormality was the cause, the Countess had Eleanore examined; she was found to have a slight sensitivity of the skin but was otherwise physically normal. The bizarre events which she witnessed were published by the Countess in Munich, 1926, in a small book called *Spuk von Talpa.*

Next, Eleanore was invited to be observed in the laboratory of Harry Price, the famous British psychical researcher. Price was convinced that the small objects he saw moving about had no physical contact with Eleanore and, in 1927, he published his report in the *Proceedings of the National Laboratory of Psychical Research.*

The Countess continued to closely watch over Eleanore; she saw the bite marks continue to appear and remained convinced that they could not have been self-inflicted. Occasionally, Eleanore's skin would be broken and bleeding, and at times the bite marks were covered with spittle. Then, in the summer of 1927, the attacks on Eleanore, as well as other poltergeist activity, ceased. The Countess had been learning about

Eleanore's past, especially focusing on her relationships with the members of her family. Having been influenced by the writings of Sigmund Freud and his theory of Psychoanalysis, the Countess became convinced that the source of the physical attacks was in Eleanore's troubled, conflicted mind. In the *British Journal of Psychical Research* of 1927, she wrote the following in an attempt to explain Eleanore's case.

"These psychical relations exactly correspond to the typical examples of hysteria according to the psychoanalytical doctrine of Professor Freud, except one further step which would have to be taken: that under certain circumstances, hysterical symptoms not only occur within the organism of the subject but that they can also attain an activity in the objective world."

Stigmata

In Eleanore's case, the specific placement of bleeding wounds on her body were referred to as "stigmatic." When such markings appear, are they the work of assaulting incubi and succubi, sexually perverse demons, or do they represent the manifestations of a deep religious ecstasy and, therefore, to be considered signs of goodness, profound religiousness, and devout faith?

The stigmata that are much like the wounds that Christ had on the cross have been appearing for centuries on the hands and feet of devout saints and religious people. In the ancient world, these marks were often inflicted on criminals and slaves with branding irons. Crucifixion was also the sentence imposed on the condemned of the Roman Empire during Christ's time and on Christ, himself, as punishment for challenging Roman authority. Among the most famous to have experienced stigmata was St. Francis of Assisi, in 1224. In 1868, a young girl, Theresa Neumann, began to have stigmatic marks appear on her hands and feet, as well as bleeding from the eyes. This occurred in the presence of witnesses, and was repeated every Good Friday. As Theresa's fame spread, she was invited to the Belgian Academy of Medicine where she was kept under close observation. It was soon discovered that the bleeding was coming from small abrasions in the skin, but since the areas of the body were sealed from possible outside contact, the mystery remained as to how the bleeding could commence.

In a more recent case, in 1918, an Italian Capuchin Monk, Padre Pio, while falling into trance as he said mass, experienced stigmatic marks. Each time thereafter, whenever he went into a deep, religiously induced trance, the stigmata would appear. While some cases of stigmata have been shown to be self-inflicted, in Padre Pio's case the Vatican investigation found no evidence of fraud, either conscious or unconscious.

The traditional school of thought is that nails were driven through the palms of Christ's hands, while more recent findings suggest to those in the religious community that the nails might have been hammered into the wrists. What if this latter view becomes accepted by very devout, religious people who, while in a state of religious ecstasy and trance, begin to have the stigmatic bleeding appear at the wrists instead of from the palms? If stigmata have their origin in the unconscious mind, then wouldn't we expect to find the wounds appearing on different places on the body depending on which historical interpretation of the crucifixion of Christ is believed? Will this change demonstrate that a person's beliefs determine where that stigmata will appear, therefore proving that we are observing the physical, unconscious manifestations of the mind rather than the results of an external force acting on the body?

Alternative explanations abound, and the debate and controversy continue.

Conclusions

For thousands of years we have heard stories of spirits and demons interacting with humans of our world and dimension. Reports continue of unseen forces that act upon the bodies of men, women, and children to inflict sexual torment, visible wounds, and even psychological turmoil. The investigation of the incubi and succubi of folklore, as well as the recently well-documented and observed cases of mysterious poltergeist activity, has moved into the scientist's laboratory. Will evidence finally emerge to demonstrate the truth of one theory over another? Is the traditional view correct that spirits or entities from another dimension are the causes, or have poltergeists been found to be the recurrent spontaneous psychokinesis flowing out of an unconscious agent's living body?

In an interview given in 1993 by Hans Holzer, the world-renowned parapsychologist, another view was suggested. Holzer, the author of more than two dozen books on the subject, has come to believe that human personality survives the death of the body, and if death comes unexpectedly, as a result of a sudden accident for example, that part which survives death continues in this earthly dimension in a confused, traumatized psychological state. The "ghost" that remains is usually emotionally upset and unaware of what to do now that it is separated from its physical body.

While this ghost is usually invisible to the living, it desperately seeks help from the living. Because it usually cannot be heard, it makes itself felt by scratching and biting and physically assaulting some poor, unsuspecting person, all in an effort to get attention and help. Holzer believes that these incubi-succubi attacks are not perpetrated by demons or evil entities, but rather by the ghosts of people who have died traumatically and who are now seeking help from the living.

When Holzer worked with Sybil Leek, who has since passed on, he would make contact with the ghost through Mrs. Leek, who would, in trance, serve as a medium. He would then try to help the ghost to the realization that it was time to move on from this dimension of existence to that in which it now belonged. A "ghost," according to Holzer, is to be distinguished from a "spirit"; a spirit is that which survives the body's death and with full awareness moves on to the dimension which is its next realm of existence. When we find ourselves under ghostly attack, now armed with this understanding, we should abandon fear and react with compassion for the ghost. Therefore, according to Holzer, if you suddenly find yourself under siege, talk to the entity, explaining that "this is now my house; call out to your loved ones to help you and take you away."

Given the plethora of theories that abound about the true nature of incubi-succubi, ghosts and spirits, demons and angels, is there one view of reality that has earned our belief and trust? Or is the universe much more complicated than any of us has imagined, and therefore all of the above theories have some truth in them, with one theory applying to one set of cases and other theories more appropriately explaining others? We suspect that the discoveries of the next several decades may surprise us with facts and theories that, due to the limits of our present knowledge, we cannot even guess at nor imagine!

CHAPTER 5

Margo: A Case of an Incubus Attack ?

THE INTERVIEW WITH MARGO EVOLVED IN A roundabout way. A student in Phil Stander's parapsychology class reported that he knew a woman "who knew a woman" who had experienced some dramatic poltergeist phenomena. This statement was not one that aroused high hopes for interesting paranormal material. Usually, this twice-removed individual cannot be located, or, if found, produces material of little interest, like scratching sounds in the attic of a (squirrel infested?) house. Nevertheless, we followed up on the lead and were finally successful in locating our poltergeist lady. Margo lived, conveniently enough, in a nearby Brooklyn neighborhood. Yes, she would be willing to be interviewed, and, yes, she would also allow a tape recording of the session.

The meeting took place in Phil's office at the college. Also present was Fran, Margo's long-time friend, who had served as the student's contact. To our relief, Margo appeared to be a credible witness. She was an attractive woman in her mid-forties, with a slender body build, auburn hair, and dark eyes. She wore jewelry of the long, dangling kind, and a dark blue dress that coordinated nicely with a gray sweater. Without being loud or flamboyant, she conveyed a strong emotional intensity. She spoke in a well-controlled voice, but again tended to be emotionally expressive. She presented herself as a working woman who was able to face the daily hassles of life in Brooklyn without illusions. She told us that she did not have much formal education, but did a lot of reading on her own.

The preliminaries included some light conversation, a discussion of Margo's apparent high energy level, and a testing of the tape recorder. Once under way, Margo told us that she was accustomed to having "crazy," meaning paranormal, experiences. She was born in Brooklyn, but had no recollections of her early years there, since her family moved to Miami when she was two years old. Although of the Jewish faith, her parents were not particularly devout, and Margo received little religious training. In fact, her father was an atheist who showed no interest in spiritual matters. On the other hand, Margo's mother reported a number of ESP experiences, usually taking the form of precognitive dreams. The family was not financially secure, especially during Margo's early years. They lived in a run-down section of South Miami and moved frequently to new rooms and hotels. The father was a sometimes bookmaker who tried various other business ventures. The family's fortunes improved during Margo's teen years. Margo returned to New York at age seventeen. Between ages seventeen and twenty-one, she lived as a single parent raising her young son. She married at age twenty-one, but the marriage lasted only for a brief period. She worked as a waitress to support herself and her son.

Margo told us that she was accustomed to having paranormal experiences. In fact, they had occurred so often in her life that she had learned not to overreact to them. For example, at age five, she crawled out on the roof of a private home where she resided with her family in Florida. She slipped and felt herself falling over the edge. Panic was arrested when a pair of firm hands held her from below and pushed her back up to safety. When she turned, there was no one to be seen.

In addition, Margo had a number of precognitive dreams, and seemed to be the center of mischievous poltergeist events. Windows opened and closed without obvious cause, lights flicked on and off, and there were mysterious sounds in her living quarters.

In her early twenties, she moved to an apartment in Brooklyn. From the vacant apartment above, after the death of the old lady who had lived there, Margo began to hear the sounds of footsteps. It seemed to her that these sounds were identical to the ones the old lady made when she was still alive. Far from being alarmed, she felt reassured by the familiar footsteps. Margo's paranormal experiences were usually of this benign type. It was partly for this reason that she was totally unprepared for the entrance of a malevolent force into her life.

The incubus experience took place three years later when she was living in the three-room apartment in Brooklyn. Her son was asleep in the bedroom while she was dozing on the living room couch, clad only in a lace nightgown. Her friend Fran had called earlier, and they briefly discussed some odd events that had occurred the night before in Margo's apartment. Fran had been conscious of strange shadows in the foyer of the apartment, and observed that a window had closed by itself.

We continue the story as it was told to Phil in Margo's own words:

Margo: Okay—this was a time in my life I had just pulled twenty-four. At that time I was fairly unproductive, but I did read a lot. I had a son that was mischievous and was six. I was living in a three-room apartment. I had a friend that lived across the hall from me who was a dog—this is interesting too, that I had made great friends with this dog and this dog was very, believe it or not, protective of me. Now, as I was saying, all my life I had crazy experiences, that is why a lot of times I didn't have fear in a lot of situations where people would have fear. I just knew there was nothing that was going to happen to me at that time. Okay, and also at that time I'd been doing a lot of reading, as I said before, and I had come up with this great theory. You know, being a very sacrilegious [sic] person, having no formalized training of religion, I had been reading at that time a lot of Herman Hesse and they had the God of Good and Evil, Abraxes. Okay—so I came up with this great theory that maybe people have the wrong God. So at times in my musings when I had nothing better to do I would pray to the devil—I'd let things go, well I would certainly not ask it to rule the world or anything evil and I didn't think of this [as] anything too seriously, it was just another joke to me because I'm one of these people that will accept most anything and believe in absolutely nothing.

Professor: What apartment were you in? Did you say the first floor?

Margo: Yes, it was the first floor—my son slept in the bed-room and I slept in the living room. I had a Hi-riser that I slept on. The front of it faced the foyer and okay and so that is more or less it.

Professor: You and your son lived together?

Margo: Yes, absolutely and it never bothered him when strange things happened either. You know he couldn't care less, you know to him it was life. These things happened if we were walking by and something dropped—so what! Okay, but interestingly enough my son was a very light sleeper. I could always get this kid up like this (snap of finger). Fran had come over the night before and had told me about the window and she was laughing. I mean for her to be hyster-ical she said "Oh! by the way your window just closed!"

Fran: But then you would even see hands go by.

Margo: She saw things I didn't and if I did see it I'd seen so much of this garbage that I just blocked things out—I absolutely blocked it out.

Fran: It wasn't by the window or a head popping up. There were shadows in this little maybe four-foot foyer and you would just see it flying by.

Margo: It never bothered me—I was not the type to have nightmares or anything like that. I remember it was the night before now—the next night I had taken a nap or something and it was about from nine to ten o'clock and Fran called me at ten o'clock and she said okay you were sleeping, I said yeah, but you got me up and blah, blah, and we spoke for about five minutes. Now I was trying to get back to sleep and I was still conscious, because I was remembering the conversation—okay I'm laying down and this is interesting because I was lying on my back and my arms were open, my legs were open and I was totally relaxed—my mouth was open!! Okay and suddenly I heard the door slam violently—now this was the scary part, I thought I was being robbed and I said "Oh! you dummy you forgot to lock the door!" I said "just pretend you're asleep and maybe this person won't kill you." I felt it coming closer—it took about three seconds for me to realize it was coming closer. I felt it coming closer and closer, I knew it was coming close but I didn't yet hear footsteps. I was still saying they're coming to rob me and I'm going to pretend I'm asleep and I was trying to roll myself up in a ball in a fetal position. Suddenly, then I was grabbed by both my legs; this force lifted my legs off the bed. I think the only thing touching was this part of my back—my arms were flung out—this force was so strong it banged on me right here (top of chest) forcing my mouth open and it smelled awful and went down my throat. I sometimes think it maybe was orally or something. I don't know because my legs were open also and I remember the hairs on the nape of my neck standing out. Now I know what an erection is like. The hairs on my arms they went straight up and I felt every hair on my body rise and the stench of it—it was like a deep, smelly—a sour smell from deep in the earth. Not a human smell. Not that I ever had my nose to damp earth but I know this is how it smells. I remember trying to fight it—to fight it, and slowly then it took the bolster. And I remember now ... the bolster from the hi-riser went on my chest.

Professor: Probably to hold you down?

Margo: Yes, now this whole time I had not opened my eyes I realized. I did not know what I was thinking consciously; my only thought was to survive. However, something made me realize I could not open my eyes.

Fran: Remember the purple mark on your throat?

Margo: Something made me realize that I cannot open my eyes because if I see this I will die of a heart attack. I knew it wouldn't look like Edmund Gwynne.

Professor: But did you ever—did your eyes open a crack?

Margo: No, no, I fought it with my eyes closed—that brave I wasn't.

Professor: All the time from beginning to end?

Margo: Yes because of the smell and it was awful.

Professor: Yeah, as if your mouth was so you couldn't scream because it was inside of you. Were you able to breathe?

Margo: I don't remember.

Fran: No you weren't—that is what you told me, you had trouble breathing.

Margo: I just remember that horrible thing. It's like when you're terrified, you will fight.

Professor: That is survival.

Margo: Yeah, it's like you're conscious, but you're not. I don't think I was forming words in my mind— like saying this is happening to me.

Professor: What were you wearing at the time, nothing?

Margo: No I think I was wearing a little lace thing.

Professor: Okay how do we say this? ... a house dress?

Margo: It was probably a little longer than a "baby doll," you know with little lace puff sleeves and a little bow.

Professor: Okay—go to the next step. Now your body is up in the air.

Margo: My legs are open, it's like it was pulling me apart, it's like being drawn and quartered. But yet I felt no hands. I only felt this force.

Professor: It was a force—nothing like hands or ropes?

Margo: No and finally I was trying to get myself together again because if I could get myself together I could close off and finally little by little I seemed to be winning. Okay, this gave me great courage.

Professor: How long was the whole episode?

Margo: It could have been five to seven minutes. To me it took forever.

Professor: Five to seven minutes is a long time.

Margo: Because every time I relive it, it becomes more frightening. It ended so gradually: this is the frightening part. First my hands were slowly released, my legs were very slowly coming together and it came out of my throat ... it was the very very last thing.

Professor: Wait a minute, you were penetrated in two places, right?

Margo: I didn't feel the penetration between my legs or ...

Professor: Oh! so you never felt the penetration, just the oral penetration—that is the difference.

Margo: So I don't—unless there were two of them.

Professor: It was oral penetration only.

Margo: Even though the legs were open and the arms were spread apart and the bolster—that was to keep me pinned.

Fran: ... even with her legs up and her arms spread.

Margo: But I remember my legs were up in the air like I felt myself half in the air—it was like I was defying gravity.

Professor: Oh! I got it. I understand what you are saying.

Margo: It gradually, gradually, left me and it finally came out of my mouth and I still felt the cold in the back of my neck.

Professor: Where did that cold come from?

Margo: It was very cold and it was very wet and moist even though my skin did not feel wet and moist ... if my skin was moist, it was from sweat.

Professor: But where did the wet and moist come from—was that all over your body or was that wet feeling just in your mouth?

Margo: No, on my body I just felt the terrible cold.

Professor: Oh! so that was it, you felt cold?

Margo: Yes.

Professor: Oh! It was the back of your neck right? Limited to the back of your neck.

Margo: That was where the main sensation was—I was so attacked, I was so opened to everything, so totally helpless that I could only feel that horrible penetration down my throat.

Fran: Could it be that the whole aura of it was just encircling you?

Margo: Perhaps and that was the last to leave me and it gradually went away and the door slammed again.

Professor: You heard the door open, and then slam closed?

Margo: First I laid there and as soon as it was over I was not frightened—I felt the adrenalin flying—I felt like superman, I felt very strong.

Professor: Adrenalin going—did I leave anything out, temperature change, we have the feeling of the skin—superman, yes the presence of several—not just one or is the feeling of just one or is it two?

Margo: Well I always felt there was something else holding me.

Professor: Something holding you and something penetrating.

Margo: Yes—that seems the best way of describing it.

Professor: What happened after it left?

Margo: After I felt sure it was gone, I sat up and looked around. I felt very strong and in control. I had grappled with the unknown and survived. It was a heady feeling ...

like ... with waves of adrenalin running through me. Then, I thought of my young son and ran to his room. He was in a deep sleep. I called his name as I tried to shake him awake. I put on the light, ran to the closet, and began to get dressed. This was difficult because I was shaking uncontrollably. I glanced into the mirror over the dresser and noticed a purple bruise the size of a quarter about two inches down from my throat. I picked up my child and carried him from his room. Somehow, I managed to switch on every light as I went through the apartment. Brightness was sanity to me. When I approached the door ... to my utter disbelief ... I found it to be securely bolted. The realization that the door had been locked all the time made me feel queasy to the pit of my stomach. It told me what I already knew that the thing—I didn't know what to call it—was some kind of disembodied spirit.

Professor: Where did you go after you left the apartment?

Margo: I ran upstairs and left my son—who was sort of dazed—in the care of neighbors. I felt terrified as though it was still there in the hallway. I ran downstairs and out of the building. I must have gotten to Fran's place by cab. ... It was sort of a blur.

Fran: When she came in, she was in a state of shock. She told me what happened. Then we were both scared. We left the lights on all night. There was a feeling ... as though it might still be present, although we didn't see anything.

Margo: By the next morning, I felt better pretty much recovered.

When Margo returned to her apartment, all was quiet. The entity, whatever it was, was gone. She noticed that a Mazzuza which had been mounted on the wall seemed to have disappeared. Later, a neighbor told her that her dog had "gone insane" during the night, barking and screaming. This dog was a "friend" to Margo and she wondered if it had been somehow aware of her strange visitor.

After Margo had told of her experience, we asked questions about the nature of the entity that had assaulted her, but she was not able to be very specific. It seemed to be a powerful force, but not completely overpowering, since she had been able to resist it. If it had human form, it would have required two entities to do what it did to her body. No, she had never experienced anything like it prior to this night, and never did again. Yes, she had a number of subsequent experiences that were inexplicable, but none involved a malevolent force. She felt that the experience was in a way beneficial to her. It seemed that she had come through a trial by fire unhurt and stronger than before. Since we ran out of time before Margo could answer all of our questions, it was decided to continue at a later date.

The next meeting included only Margo and the two authors of this book. The general purpose was to determine if the events described by Margo could be explained in a rational way. For example, we asked about Margo's use of drugs such as LSD, which was much in vogue during the late 1960s. Margo answered that she was essentially "straight" during her youth, admitting only to occasional use of pot. In any case, there had been no use of any drugs for months prior to the incident. In a similar vein, Margo denied any prior hallucinatory experiences.

In response to questions, Margo denied being frustrated about her sexual life at the time of the incident. In fact, she did not experience any sexual feelings during the attack. Although it was a kind of rape, the attack was not primarily sexual in nature. It seemed as though the demon wanted to enter her in the sense of wanting to possess her. The thing entered her mouth and seemed to be searching or probing for something. There was no vaginal penetration.

In response to questions about her spiritual life at the time of the attack, Margo admitted that she sometimes speculated about the relation between God and the Devil. She sometimes wondered if the two weren't the same. She sometimes prayed to the devil, but this was done in a less than serious way. At no time was she involved in any organized religious group or cult. In fact, she reported spending little time thinking about spiritual matters.

Margo's story follows much of the pattern of the "Incubus rape" reported for hundreds of years: classically, a woman is alone in her room when a foul-smelling demon, usually invisible, pins her down and rapes her brutally, sometimes again and again. In some accounts, the attack occurs in the presence of others who struggle against the unseen demon while, before their eyes, bruises and cuts appear on the victim's body. Typically, the woman is being violated by so powerful a force that others cannot help her.

In Margo's case, a number of elements are present: her sense of a putrid-smelling entity, its great power used in pinning her down against her will, the bruise on her chest, and the way in which her arms and legs were spread apart in a position of ultimate vulnerability. Perhaps the most unusual feature of the case is the oral penetration. While the penetration was deep, she was never so completely possessed that she lost her will or her spirit, but how are parapsychologists working in the rational world of scientific method to make sense of this? After all, many in the scientific community do not accept the reality of ESP, despite the fact that both the Pentagon and Soviet Union have spent millions of dollars in the last decade in its investigation. To ask already skeptical scientists to entertain the reality of ESP, PK, and then ghosts is to put a great strain on their credulity. Nevertheless, a sober, bright individual has presented us with a spontaneous experience that defies testing in the laboratory, and it is a tale told so often that it should not be dismissed without an attempt at explanation.

Let's look at some possible explanations for Margo's report. Is it plausible that an act of fraud has been perpetrated, and that the tale is a conscious fabrication? We don't think so because Margo has nothing to gain from telling her story. Even her name has been changed in this retelling to assure her anonymity. Was Margo's experience a dream or hallucination? Margo rejects any such suggestion in the light of her stable lifestyle, and in view of the fact that she never had any previous or subsequent occurrences. If the entity was a product of her unconscious mind, why did she experience it once and only once? We are also at a loss to account for the bruise which appeared on her chest. If she were dreaming, why didn't the intense pressure on her chest awaken her? If there are disembodied spirits that either survive the death of the body or dwell in some other dimension, and occasionally intrude into our own, how can we come to understand them, given the limitations of our scientific technology? Such limitations should not close our minds and prevent us from raising the necessary questions.

CHAPTER 6

Famous British Cases

THE BRITISH ISLES HAVE PROVIDED US WITH SUCH a great wealth of material that we were able to pick and choose from the many reported cases. (About half of the 500 cases cited by Alan Gauld and A. D. Cornell in their book, *Poltergeists,* originated in England, Scotland, Ireland, or Wales.) Clearly, we needed some basis to guide us in selecting, and so we adopted A. R. G. Owen's definition of "evidential" cases: these are "cases in which literate and respectable witnesses have supplied written accounts free from internal contradiction" (*Can We Explain the Poltergeist?* 1964). The cases selected, then, were restricted to those in which at least one independent eyewitness observed the phenomenon and provided a written account. In fact, there were multiple witnesses to some of the cases selected. A second criterion was met in that we selected cases that are different from one another, thereby representing different kinds of poltergeist events.

Although cases had been reported earlier, it is only during the late 1500s that reliable firsthand narratives began to appear. As the years went by, the study of poltergeists began to be conducted in a scientific spirit. Our first British case, dating from 1591, is an early example of a study that was conducted in a spirit of skeptical investigation.

The North Aston Poltergeist

The details of this case are described in an anonymous pamphlet published in London in 1592 and titled, *A True Discourse of Such Straunge and Woonderfull Accidents, as happened in the House of M. George Lee of North Aston, in the County of Oxford, being in truth and matter of such special weight and consequence, as sildome hath the like bene heard of before, which begun the 19 of November 1591 ...*

We are indebted to Alan Gauld for his work in tracking down this pamphlet and publishing parts of it in his book, *Poltergeists* (1979). He also provided some historical data about the Lee family. George Lee of North Aston, whose farmhouse was the scene of the activity, was one of two children of Edward Lee, the other being a sister, Anne. It may be that the author of the pamphlet received much of the information from Edward Lee, who died about two years after the cessation of the events. In any case, George Lee was a single man of twenty-one when the events began.

We will not quote from the pamphlet verbatim so that you need not translate the archaic spelling in which it was written. In summary, the pamphlet begins with the statement that on

November 29, 1591, George observed a shower of stones falling on the roof of his "Hall." The stones ranged from one to twenty-two pounds in weight, and seemed to be violently flung at the house. He continued to be completely amazed by the series of what appeared to be strange events, and conducted a diligent search to find the causes of the stone throwing. With the help of others, George closely examined the interior and exterior of the house, but they could find nothing wrong with the tiles or slates of the roof, and could detect no sign of trickery or illusion. No one was able to offer a reasonable explanation of where the stones came from.

Meanwhile, the stones continued to fall throughout December and into the next year. The unexplained events were witnessed by numerous neighbors, workers, and also by Mr. Giles, the vicar, all of whom kept watch at the house at one time or another. The date is uncertain, but at some point the Lees decided to live elsewhere.

However, Edward Lee wanted someone to stay in the house and let him know when the stone falling came to an end. The author of the pamphlet tells us that one day Edward sent his young daughter, Anne, accompanied by a servant maid, Joan, to spend the night there. However, when they heard the stones slamming against the walls, they did not get beyond the front gate. They retreated and agreed to try again, at which time they were escorted by three of Lee's workmen. When the five arrived at a little court before the door, they heard the sound of stones violently hitting the walls of the house. One of the workers boldly opened the door and plainly saw the falling of stones. He led the others upstairs to investigate one of the rooms where they observed two falling stones, one of which knocked loose a rod that held up a curtain, possibly belonging to a four-poster.

The North Aston case is one of those in which there is no single agent whose presence is needed to stimulate the events. Two men, who apparently visited the house when no family members were present, gave the following report. They were in the house for a long while and had seen nothing unusual when one of them in jest asked the poltergeist to "fling us down a quoit or two," so that they might play a game. (Quoits was a game commonly played in the fields with a thin, broad stone). A round quoit, in exactly the form and shape of the type of stone used in the game, suddenly fell to the ground. The men jokingly asked for another such stone, and their wish was immediately gratified. And when they asked for two more, two more dropped down. They inspected the stones and found that one of them had been marked in such a way to confirm that it had in fact been used to play the game.

On the following day, Edward Lee, accompanied by two young men and two servant girls, went to spend the night at the farm. When nothing happened by 2 A.M., he sent the two men home. Later, Joan, one of the servants, reported that she had been assailed with stones, and that the cover on which Edward lay had been pulled from his bed. A number of strange events followed. They found the window of one of the bedrooms open with a sword thrust through the window and hanging by the hilt. In the morning, they found that two bolsters had been taken from a bed in the parlor and thrown on the floor. Mr. Lee marked the outline of the bolsters on the floor as they lay. The bolsters were then returned to the bed on which they belonged. Mr. Lee and servants left the room for the parlor and, upon their return, found that the chalk marks had been wiped out. This experiment was repeated with fresh chalk marks, but this time the door to the room was locked. They returned to the room half an hour later and found the chalk wiped out again. A third repetition of this experiment had an unexpected result. This time, they observed that the chalk marks were intact but they found two designs cut into the floor, one resembling a bear's paw, and the other a hawk's talons.

A lull in the strange events began after January 6, 1592, but on February 15, the stone throwing began again in a "more fierce" manner than before. As the fame of these events spread throughout the area, various people, including the sheriff, came to see for themselves. New phenomena were reported, including the appearance of drops of blood on the hall table, and the appearance of the house lit up as if there were a fire, as well as the apparitions of strange or grotesque animals.

The events came to a sad end in May of 1592 when young George Lee ended his life. Following his burial on May 22, nothing at all of an unusual nature was seen or heard.

Alan Gauld speculated that the author of the pamphlet got the story directly from eyewitnesses, and noted that their accounts seem to be largely consistent with one another. It may be that the events at North Aston were due to some complicated conspiracy of the Lees' servants and workers. If this were so, many must have been involved because different persons were present at various times. Nor is there a clue as to what the conspirators would hope to gain by staging such a circus of events. Gauld concluded that the author's story has a certain ring of truth, the most convincing evidence being that certain events occurred inside locked rooms in what might be considered an early attempt at controlled observation. Certainly, the stone-throwing poltergeist represents a type of case that was to be reported again and again in later times. One of the most famous collectors of stone falls stories, as well as the falling of frogs and fish and raining blood, was Charles Fort. Such works as *Book of the Damned* (originally published in 1921, included in *The Complete Works of Charles Fort*, Dover, New York, 1975), related many such anecdotes, often without analysis or explanation, letting the "facts," or anecdotes speak for themselves. To this day, in circles where the paranormal is discussed, these bizarre occurrences are referred to as "Fortean Phenomena."

The Bristol Poltergeist

Cases involving poltergeists that assault or physically injure their victims are relatively uncommon. Nevertheless, a number of such instances have been reported; these involve the victim being bitten, scratched, dragged about, their belongings torn to shreds, hit with stones or excrement, and, in one case, apparently murdered. The Bristol case is one of the earliest, well-documented accounts of an assaultive poltergeist, beginning in November 1761 and going on to December of the next year. A detailed account titled, *A narrative of some extraordinary things that happened to Mr. Richard Gile's children,* was published in Bristol in 1800, the year after the author's death. The author, Henry Durbin, did not publish the story in his lifetime, partly because he had been abused in the public papers when he first looked into the situation. He believed that he lived in an age when "men scoff at spiritual things." If they did not believe in Moses or Christ, he argued, why should they believe in his feeble testimony?

The Durbins were a prominent family in the area, and Harry was a respected and well-to-do druggist. A friend who wrote the preface to the book described Henry as a man of "unblemished uprightness" known for his charity, honesty, and piety to God. However, he was by no means a gullible man. In fact, when he first heard of the strange events at the Lamb's Inn at Lawford's Gate, he went "to detect and expose what he deemed to be imposture." However, after many months of careful research, he came away freely convinced that the events were due to some supernatural agency. It should be noted that Henry Durbin was not the only person to investigate this case. Several clergymen and other well-known citizens also studied the situation firsthand and could find no evidence of fraud.

The events centered on the two daughters of innkeeper Mr. Richard Giles: Dobby, who was eight years old, and Molly, who was thirteen. The first disturbances were scratching and rapping sounds that were especially noticeable in the girls' bedroom. The sounds became stronger and continued throughout the entire period of the disturbance. The phenomena began to attract outside attention and had been in progress for several weeks when Durbin made his first visit during December 1761. He was so impressed by what he witnessed that he came by on a daily basis and made notes on his observations. Here are his first observations in his own words: "18 Dec. 1761, hearing that Mr. Giles' children, Miss Molly and Dobby, were afflicted in an extraordinary manner for a fortnight past, I went there this day, and saw Molly sewing, and she had marks on her arm given on a sudden, like the marks of a thumbnail; which I am satisfied she could not do herself. As I watched her, I saw the flesh pressed down whitish, and rise again, leaving the print of a fingernail, the edges of which grew red afterwards. The girl complained that it... hurted her much, and smarted often."

Mr. Giles told Durbin that he originally thought the strange noises were tricks of the servants. At five A.M., on a previous day, Mr. Giles was disturbed by violent scratching and knocking sounds coming from the girls' bedroom. He entered the children's room expecting to catch servants in the act. Instead, he observed the cover of a box move up and down several times, apparently without cause. The cover moved again and fell to the ground of its own accord. Then the box, which contained the children's clothes, moved several times, then turned over, spilling the contents on the floor. Later that night, the father saw a hanger pulled from Molly's hand by some unseen force and thrown on the floor. Molly claimed that she could see the hand that was tormenting her. Mr. Giles was startled by these events and was soon convinced of their supernatural origin.

One of the more amazing events took place early the following year and was observed by Mr. Durbin, who reported as follows: "On the chest of drawers stood a wine glass which I saw glitter in the sun, and was astonished to see it rise ... without hands. It rose gradually about a foot perpendicularly from the drawers; then the glass seemed to stand, and thereupon inclined backwards, as if a hand had held it; it was then thrown with violence about five feet and struck the nurse on the hip a hard blow." He added that no one was near the glass when it rose. The children who were standing near him ran to the other end of the room, "fearing that it would be flung at them, as things generally were ..."

On January 6, the two girls were attacked in front of numerous witnesses. Mr. Durbin reported that the girls were bitten about twenty times that evening while they lay in bed with their arms in full view. They could not have done it themselves with observers present. "We examined the bites," said Mr. Durbin, "and found on them the impression of eighteen or twenty teeth, with saliva or spittle all over them, and the spittle smoking [sic], as if just spit out of the mouth. I took some of it on my finger ... and Mr. _____ did the same, and we found it clammy ... and it smelt rank."

Later, Molly complained that her arm had been rubbed with nasty stuff. About a teacupful of spittle was found on her arm in a lather. This experience was repeated on subsequent occasions in front of witnesses, with the spittle sometimes appearing without bite marks.

On the seventh of January, Durbin and three witnesses were watching the girls in their bed. "It" began beating and scratching them as it often did, and then proceeded to bite them, leaving the spittle on the bite. It appeared obvious to the witnesses that the girls were bitten on their backs and shoulders while on their backs "which put it out of doubt they did not do it themselves." The children were screaming in pain, and the gentlemen attempted to protect them, covering their arms and hands with a petticoat. Not only was this tactic a failure, it actually seemed to make things worse. When the petticoat was removed, fresh deep bites were evident with accompanying slime. The teeth left an impression in the flesh, oval in shape and about two inches in length. On a later occasion, Durbin was talking to Dobby when she cried out that she was bitten in the neck. Again, Durbin concluded that she could not have done it herself since she was marked on the top of the shoulder out of reach of her mouth.

The girls were also repeatedly pricked with pins that had been taken from their clothes or from pincushions they carried with them. The pins were generally bent into extravagant shapes, prompting Mr. Durbin to begin to collect them. Durbin, smarting from criticisms appearing in the public newspapers, arranged the following experiment in the hope of convincing the world that the events were genuinely paranormal. He made Molly sit down in the chair in the middle of the parlor in front of witnesses. He asked her to cross her hands and sit still while he marked a large pin at the top. He put the pin in her pincushion, and inserted the pincushion in her pocket and pulled her clothes over it while the observers watched her closely. Almost immediately she cried out and was pricked in the neck with her hands still folded. The marked pin was run through her shirt and stuck in the skin of her neck. The pin had been curiously bent. The experiment was repeated with four other pins. Again, within half a minute, the pins were stuck in her neck and all were bent. The pins were no longer in the pincushion.

An interesting feature of the case was its relationship to the witchlore of the previous century. It is apparent from Durbin's account that belief in witches was alive and well in the England of 1761. Durbin detected signs of intelligent communication in the rappings that usually came from the girls' bedroom. Beginning on January 23, 1762, Durbin began to communicate with a spirit who identified herself as a witch from Mangotsfield in Gloucestershire, who had been hired for money by Mr. Giles' rival carriers. The fact that several of Mr. Giles' wagons broke down for no good reason seemed to support the story. Several months later, Mr. Giles caught sight of a boy standing by his carriage, an event that was thought to be related to his death shortly thereafter. The witch-spirit stated more or less accurately that she would have power over the children for another forty weeks from the first communication in late January. Durbin reported that the spirit was able to answer questions posed in Latin and Greek, and also would respond to thought questions. Occasionally, the spirit communicated by voice, often in an abusive tone. These scurrilous remarks were on some occasions heard by all present, according to Durbin. When it appeared that the troubles were continuing beyond the predicted period, Mrs. Giles decided to take matters into her own hands. She visited a "cunning woman" at Bedminster who seemed very familiar with the details of the case. She advised Mrs. Giles to perform the following ceremony: "Take the two children's first water in the morning," and put it in a pipkin on the fire and boil it; "and if, when it boiled, all colours of the rainbow came out of it visibly, she could cure it ...." The ceremony was performed according to instructions, and beautiful rainbow colors came out of the pot. From that day, the strange events at Lamb's Inn came to an end.

To modern readers, the witchcraft aspects of the case tend to reduce its credibility. Even at the time, many skeptical persons believed the events to be fraudulent. One historian advanced the theory that the events were staged by Mrs. Giles to depreciate the value of the house which her mother wanted to buy. In their book, *Poltergeists* (1979), Gauld and Cornell stated that this theory was based on gossip and "can have no standing against a first-hand narrative of personal experiences." They also noted that the strange events were not centered on the house but on the two girls. When Molly and Dobby were removed to other houses, the phenomena followed them there, making it obvious that "it was the two children who were haunted and not the house." It should be kept in mind that the validity of the phenomena did not depend on a belief in witchcraft. It could be that the strange events, observed by so many witnesses, actually occurred, and that Durbin's interpretation of the events was invalid.

Another possible interpretation of the physical assault, discussed by Gauld and Cornell, is that the two girls were "hysterics," meaning that they unconsciously converted underlying states of emotional conflict into bodily disorders. It is well known that certain sensitive persons may produce marks and skin injuries under hypnosis or by means of autosuggestion. For example, many cases have been reported of sensitive persons who have suffered the stigmata of Christ, cuts on the forehead and bleeding of the palms of the hands, under conditions in which there was no apparent external cause. We do not know much about the emotional lives of the girls in this case. It is clear that if the wounds were in any way self-induced, the girls must have felt an inordinate need for punishment. Durbin tells us that at one point Molly "had about forty cuts on her arms, face and neck, with the blood dried on them, and very sore. They looked very black and were all about two inches and a half long, and about the thickness of a shilling deep ...."

Even if valid, the idea that the girls were hysterics would only pertain to their physical wounds, not the poltergeist phenomena. Is it possible, however, that the emotional conflicts of the girls in some way produced the poltergeist effects? Gauld and Cornell noted that there are numerous cases in which it appears that an underlying psychological disturbance has stimulated both hysterical symptoms and poltergeist events. We will come across this interpretation again in some of the cases to be discussed in this book.

In concluding this case, we repeat that it is certainly one of the best documented of the early cases. Ultimately, one's assessment of the validity of the case rests on Mr. Durbin's credibility as a witness. We can only say that we are not aware of any information that would cast doubt on his character. He has won the support of later investigators. For example, Father Herbert Thurston, writing in his book, *Ghosts and Poltergeists* (1953), stated that "On the whole I am distinctly disposed to believe that Mr. H. Durbin was a conscientious and truthful reporter of the phenomena he claims to have witnessed."

A City of London Poltergeist

This case meets our criteria as an evidential case since there were numerous witnesses to the curious events. However, we admit to selecting it, in part, because of its comic overtones. Many of us spend part or most of our working day in or around an office; we can easily put ourselves in the place of the office workers who find their workplace has, more or less, "gone crazy." The informant was Mr. Lister Drummond who was a practicing attorney in 1901, the year of the disturbances; he tells us that the events took place in business premises in the heart of London. Father Herbert Thurston, in *Ghosts and Poltergeists,* testified that Mr. Drummond was considered a man of integrity by his peers.

We will not repeat here the glowing testimonials of his contemporaries, except to say that he was a highly regarded

Catholic who was to become a Metropolitan Police Magistrate some years after the conclusion of this case. Excerpts of Drummond's manuscript, *Account of Certain Phenomena Witnessed by Me at the Offices of the* _____," are provided by Thurston who acquired the manuscript from another clergyman who had not published it.

After lunch, during a day in January 1901, Drummond was accosted in the street by a man named Steward, who said he wanted help in regard to an urgent matter. This man was under the incorrect impression that Drummond was an experienced investigator of supernatural events. Steward referred to certain extraordinary events that had been going on for the past eighteen months at the office where he was employed as a Registrar. Various articles such as ink bottles, rulers, and blotting paper had been flying about the office in the presence of himself and his fellow clerks. Pieces of plaster had apparently been thrown from the ceiling in the corner of the room. Articles that had been under lock and key escaped from their confines and were found elsewhere, and were sometimes seen in flight. Doors opened violently when no one was near them. The accountant employed by the firm reported that a glass door opened and closed by itself when only he was in the office. These events seemed to occur without any human agency being responsible. Intrigued by this report, Drummond promised to visit the office on the following day.

On January 28, the five office workers who were present confirmed Mr. Steward's report of the previous day. They showed Drummond a tray full of various objects that had been mysteriously smashed to pieces when thrown at them by some unknown agency. Drummond and another gentleman named Keane carefully investigated the scene after hours but could find nothing out of the way. Before leaving, they placed a number of articles inside a cupboard and sealed it with red tape in such a way that the doors could be opened wide enough to see inside but not wide enough to take anything out of it. The cupboard was then locked.

On the following day, two halves of a marble letterweight that had been in the cupboard fell down in front of Steward's desk, apparently from the ceiling. The various objects that had been placed in the cupboard were now scattered about the shelves of the still-sealed cupboard. The marble objects were not inside. On the next day, Drummond and Keane broke the seals and discovered that all of the objects, once inside, had disappeared. Once again, the two investigators went about finding objects to be placed in the cupboard. As they worked, the top of a snuff box popped open by itself. They sealed the cupboard tightly this time so that it would not be possible to open the door "to the slightest degree" without breaking the seals. Nevertheless, on the following day the cupboard door burst open, with a heavy object falling out to the ground. Keane and Steward later sealed up the cupboard again, this time with a wax seal impressed with a medal featuring the heads of Saints Peter and Paul.

Steward reported that while he watched the sealed cupboard, an object descended from the top of the cupboard and struck the floor with terrific violence. It proved to be part of the marble paperweight. When Keane got a ladder to examine the top of the cupboard, the lid of a box flew open and nearly fell on him. Suddenly, objects began flying. "A succession of missiles was then showered on us from the top of the safe; portions of gas pipes, nuts and screws ..." reported Steward in a note to Drummond. Then, in the accountant's room, a perfect shower of articles descended from the ceiling—stones and pieces of quartz, copper coins, and old nails. "The situation was not without a certain sense of humor," wrote Steward, as the accountant "ran to the corner of the room for his umbrella, which he put up ...."

Things were even worse in the outer office where two workers danced from side to side to avoid the heavy missiles that were being thrown about. A blotting pad flew across the room while a chair was thrown harmlessly and with little noise. The doors of the safe slammed violently and a high stool fell over. This kind of activity went on until about 6:20 P.M. when the doors of the cupboard were flung open, with no sign of the seal or red wax evident.

Shortly thereafter, Steward found the unbroken seal of the saints on his desk. The seal was perfectly intact. All the participants remained in the office for about three hours but there were no further disturbances that night.

On February 8, Drummond observed empty tobacco tins flying about, and a heavy object was thrown down in a passageway leading to the boardroom. He watched carefully, but could detect no sign of any of the clerks having anything to do with the disturbances.

When Drummond arrived at the office on February 12, he found Keane with an umbrella up to ward off the missiles that were flying about. The office was in total confusion and no work was being done. Steward said that he had earlier locked in the accountant's iron safe an old boot that had been flying about. He was almost immediately struck in the back by the boot, having only had time to cross the room. When the men opened the safe, the boot was gone.

Years later, Father Thurston interviewed Keane, who had survived Drummond. Keane confirmed the events that his friend had described, and added that they did not pursue the case for an extended period. However, Steward informed Keane that there were notable developments months later. Specifically, the poltergeist began to communicate with the clerks orally or by raps. They asked questions of it and received answers that seemed to contain information beyond the knowledge of anyone present. The spirit further distinguished itself by communicating in an unpleasant manner, with many obscenities.

Thurston was particularly impressed by a detail in Drummond's original account. Drummond observed a tin kettle, used for making tea, fly across the room. He sketched the path of the kettle through the air and believed it was distinctly abnormal in its trajectory. This sort of event has been reported in a number of poltergeist outbreaks. Various objects, including quite heavy ones like pots and stones, have traveled through the air at strikingly slow speeds, and have been observed to fly around corners in case after case. Thurston concluded that this phenomenon "which has independently been noticed by so many observers must be real and super-normal."

A. R. G. Owen lists this as a "genuine" case in his book, *Can We Explain the Poltergeist?* (1964). Even if we accept what Drummond actually saw, it must be regarded as remarkable. Owen noted that virtually all of the fantastic activities reported in this case, including the teleportation of objects, have been asserted in other cases.

CHAPTER 7

European Cases of the Nineteenth Century

THE MOST SPECTACULAR CASES REPORTED IN CONtinental Europe during the later years of the nineteenth century involve two people: one a renowned scientist and the other a remarkable psychic. Their lives were to become intertwined as one undertook a highly publicized investigation of the other.

Introducing Cesare Lombroso

The scientist was Cesare Lombroso, a Professor of Psychiatry at Turin and director of a mental hospital, now best known for his pioneering work in a new branch of science called criminology. In his book, *L'Uomo Delinquente* (*Criminal Man,* 1909), he presented the theory that the brain of the criminal has certain primitive or atavistic features. Based on a study of prison inmates, he concluded that their brains were, in some ways, like those of cavemen. Furthermore, these tendencies were inherited, suggesting that criminals could not be expected to gain control of their antisocial tendencies. The intense controversy provoked by this theory, while interesting, is beyond the scope of this book. For present purposes, it is enough to observe that Lombroso was a hard-nosed materialist who did not believe in such concepts as "mind" and "spirit." "Yet in spite of his aggressive materialism," noted Colin Wilson, "Lombroso was too good a scientist not to be willing to study new facts" (*The Mammoth Book*).

During the 1880s, he investigated a number of baffling cases involving people who were reported to possess amazing powers. A teenage girl who could see with her ear and smell through her chin was personally studied by Lombroso. Expecting some ridiculous deception, he was amazed to find that she was able to read a letter placed near her ear, while her eyes were bandaged. At another time, her sense of smell seemed to be transposed from her nose to her foot. His reading of literature showed him that similar cases had previously been reported. There was an eleven-year-old girl who was able to hear with her elbow, and another girl was able to read a book with her stomach when her eyes were bandaged. Although he found these cases intriguing, he did not become deeply involved with these kind of phenomena until Eusapia Palladino entered his life. Lombroso was publicly challenged to investigate this remarkable woman in an open letter to a Rome journal. In spite of his fears of ridicule and the risk to his solid reputation, he decided, after years of hesitation, to undertake the investigation.

Eusapia Palladino

Eusapia was to tell the famous investigator Hereward Carrington that she had been an orphan since a young child, and had been cared for by a "family of friends." She was born in a mountain village near Bari, her mother dying shortly after her birth. Her father left her to be raised on a neighboring farm. Part of the mystique of Eusapia centered on the opening in her head that was caused by a fall when she was one year old. This cranial opening was later to become the source of a cool breeze when she was in the trance state. On the scar covering the injury there appeared a lock of white hair that remained throughout her adult years, and which became a kind of trademark.

After the death of her father when she was twelve, Eusapia was adopted by some "foreigners" living in Naples. To make a long story short, this family gave up on their efforts to educate and civilize Eusapia, who thought of herself as a wild animal, an ignorant creature who did not want to take a bath every day or to comb her hair.

Returning to friends who began arranging for her to enter a convent, Eusapia discovered her psychic talents one evening when some visitors suggested a table-turning session. With the idea of having some fun, they formed a human chain while sitting at a table. Within ten minutes, the table began to rise, the chairs began to dance, the curtains swelled, and bells began to ring. This so far exceeded their expectations that they were frightened by it "… as if in fun they had called up the devil …." However, they had the presence of mind to test each person present to find out who caused the phenomena. Of course, it was Eusapia. She was proclaimed a medium and from that time on began to give demonstrations at little seances. According to what she told Carrington, she resisted being made to sit for hours at seances, but did it only to compensate her friends for her care. She definitely did not want to go to a convent. In his book, *Eusapia Palladino and Her Phenomena* (1909), Carrington suggested that her accounts of her history were somewhat contradictory and need not be taken as gospel.

Lombroso was told that Eusapia, now thirty years old, had the power to lift articles of furniture in the air, hold them suspended, and set them down again—all by her will alone. She could increase or decease the weight of objects, produce raps, and could imprint an image on a piece of soft clay from a distance. Able to overcome the force of gravity, she could levitate her body without visible support.

According to Brian Inglis (*Natural and Supernatural*), Eusapia was also believed to be suffering from a mental disorder. Entering her trance, she often had tremors, or convulsions, and might sob or laugh maniacally. She sometimes made overt sexual advances to sitters who attracted her. As the trance deepened, she was likely to be taken over by "John King," who was her chief spirit control in Europe. In short, she exhibited many of the hysterical features of patients studied by Charcot, Janet, Breuer, and Freud. Her unstable nature created difficulties for the investigators who wanted to be strictly objective. Another aspect of her case that reduced her credibility was her well-known penchant for trickery, fraud, and deceit. Some of her efforts were incredibly clumsy and easily discovered. However, most investigators believed that she produced genuine phenomena when she was strictly controlled.

The Investigation Begins

The Milan Commission was put together to investigate Eusapia's remarkable feats in a rigorous, scientific fashion. In addition to Lombroso, the members included Giovanni Schiaparelli, director of the Milan observatory; Guiseppe Gerosa, Professor of Physics; Angelo Brofferio, a philosopher; Carl Du Prel, doctor of philosophy in Munich; Charles Richet, a physiologist by training; Alexander Aksakov, an advisor to the Emperor of Russia; and the physicist, Dr. G. B. Ermacora. This was perhaps the most distinguished group of investigators ever gathered together to study paranormal phenomena. Beginning in October 1892, meeting in the Milan apartment of M. Finzi, they carried out a long series of experiments. Seventeen sittings were carried out under varying lighting conditions—some well lit but others in near darkness.

On several occasions, under favorable lighting conditions, the investigators observed a table rise in the air in front of Eusapia when her feet were securely held down to the floor. The table rose with its four feet horizontally in the air, generally to a height of four to eight inches but occasionally to a height of about twenty-eight inches. It usually remained in the air for several seconds—long enough for the investigators to examine the four feet of the table. Good quality photographs showed the table in the air. The only problem was that Eusapia's skirt had bellied out to touch one leg of the table. The investigators were certain, however, that the skirt could not have hidden a support strong enough to lift the table.

Hereward Carrington described a further set of experiments, including the following incident: "... Professor Richet took up his station in the darkened part of the room, behind the curtains, his chair placed back to back with that on which Eusapia sat. The medium's hands were held on either side. ... Her feet were also held. Under such circumstances, however, the curtain was blown out, and Professor Richet was touched on the right shoulder by a distinct hand and pulled with some force. At the same moment, M. Finzi was touched on the ear, on the forehead, and on the temple by fingers from behind the curtain—while the hand which touched Professor Richet was free from the curtain."

In their report, the committee stated that there was no doubt that they had seen and touched a disembodied human hand on numerous occasions, under conditions when the medium's arms were visible and her hands were held by investigators on either side of her. The committee concluded that many of the results obtained during the sittings could not have been produced by trickery of any kind.

According to Brian Inglis (*Natural and Supernatural*), the Milan report was greeted by torrents of ridicule in the scientific and popular journals. Critics who had not been present believed that these distinguished scholars had been hoodwinked by a sly Italian peasant woman. In fact, only one committee member refused to sign the report. Richet took the position that conclusive proof of the genuineness of the phenomena was lacking. Conceding that he had no evidence of deception on Eusapia's part, he ended by calling for more research.

And more research there was to be. No other psychic in history was investigated by so many groups of investigators. Eusapia was investigated in Rome, Warsaw, Cambridge, Paris, and the United States. Camille Flammarion, the noted astronomer; Theodore Flournoy, Professor of Psychology;

Joseph Maxwell, author of the highly regarded *Metapsychical Phenomena;* Richard Hodgson of the Society for Psychical Research; and Hereward Carrington are just some of the noted researchers who were involved with Eusapia at one time or another.

In this brief account, we could not possibly review the findings of the many commissions that studied Eusapia, but can briefly list some of the effects she produced. It was often observed that the medium was able to move objects such as chairs, musical instruments, and tables that were out of her reach. Other effects that she often achieved were luminosities, such as hands that glowed with their own light and sometimes touched the witness. More commonly, the investigators felt themselves touched, slapped, or poked by some unseen energy. Musical instruments—a tambourine, an accordion or a zither—sounded, apparently without anyone touching them. She also was able to reduce her weight or otherwise influence scales and balances in some unexplained way. Levitations were standard fare at her seances, as were knocking and banging noises. It seems clear that many of her effects were the kind that are commonly found in poltergeist cases.

The reactions of the scholars, scientists, and professional conjurers varied greatly. Some believed that she was an out-and-out trickster. Eusapia's tendency to resort to tricks when not closely watched was well known, and provided evidence to those who doubted her. Others could not accept her obvious, clumsy cheating as in any way causing or explaining the spectacular effects she so often produced. Flournoy stated that the only possible way to achieve these results was by means of a confederate who would have access to secret doors in a room prepared in advance. Flournoy was satisfied that the control and inspections that had been carried out ruled out any such elaborate arrangements. Flammarion was not convinced by her powers until he tested her in his own home and thereby eliminated the idea that she worked with a confederate and special equipment. Other researchers admitted that they could not figure out how Eusapia did what she did, but could not bring themselves to accept observations that their intellect told them were impossible.

Eusapia Palladino lived until the 1920s, but her powers had faded, and she died in relative obscurity. As Brian Inglis recounts, she was victimized by exposés written by men who had no direct knowledge of her work and simply repeated the words of past critics. Flammarion observed that psychical research seemed to be a "no win" situation; the better the experiments, the more likely it was that positive results would be written off by academics as due to fraud or collusion between researcher and medium.

Lombroso and the Wine Shop Poltergeist

This case involved Signor Fumero, the owner of a wine shop in Turin, Italy. Bottles of wine smashed themselves and various household articles were observed to fly across the room. The police were summoned, but far from being sympathetic, they threatened Fumero with dire consequences if this nonsense did not stop at once. Fumero then concocted the story that the famous Professor Lombroso had visited the house, and, somehow, induced the noisy, destructive ghost to depart. Fumero was highly embarrassed when Lombroso, having heard reports of the infestation, visited the scene incognito. When he learned of his visitor's true identity, Fumero admitted that he lied about the end of the disturbances to keep off sightseers. In fact, the poltergeist was as active as ever, as Lombroso could see for himself whenever he would go down to the cellar.

As Colin Wilson continued the story (*The Mammoth Book*), the two men descended a flight of stairs, walked along a lengthy passageway, and entered the deep wine cellar. The noise of smashing glass was clearly audible, and some bottles struck Lombroso's foot. "And as Lombroso stood there," Wilson recounted, "three empty bottles began to spin across the floor, and shattered against the leg of a table that stood in the middle of the cellar." Signs of previous activity in the form of broken bottles lay scattered about below the shelves. With the aid of six lighted candles, Lombroso meticulously checked all the full bottles on the shelves to make sure that there were no wires or threads attached. He watched bottles leave the shelves and fall slowly to the ground. This is typical of the unusual movements and trajectories of flying objects that are so often reported in poltergeist outbreaks. According to A. R. G. Owen (*Can We Explain the Poltergeist?*), an accountant named Pierre Merino testified that he had seen both empty and full bottles cracking, then breaking, and the fragments continuing to crumble. The phenomena could not be explained as due to fermentation of the wine. Lombroso assumed that this was a poltergeist infestation, as opposed to a haunting. He expected that it would be limited in duration, and that someone on the premises was the causative agent. Just as Eusapia seemed able to cause a wide range of effects including knocking noises and levitations, someone here was supplying the energy for the disturbances.

Lombroso suspected Signor Fumero's neurotic wife of being the medium, and arranged for her to be sent on a short vacation. During her absence nothing unusual happened, but the activity started again when she returned. To make sure that she was definitely the cause of the troubles, he asked her to leave once again. This time the disturbances continued in her absence. Items of apparel floated about the house, and plates and bottles exploded in the kitchen.

The second return of Signora Fumero did nothing to alter the ongoing confusion. Since it now appeared that she was not responsible for the events, Lombroso continued his investigation, finally settling on a young man of thirteen who worked in the kitchen as a potboy. This pubescent youngster had recently undergone a growth spurt and was unusually tall. Upon his being dismissed from service, the poltergeist events abruptly ceased. Lombroso could find no particular abnormalities in the boy and assumed that his high energy level caused the events at the wine shop at 6 Via Brava. A. R. G. Owen commented that the date of the case, 1900, was an auspicious warning that "the twentieth century was to be no more free of poltergeists than less scientific eras."

Lombroso's Conclusions

Lombroso's ideas evolved over the years: from strict materialism to a final belief in spirits. He was looking for some way to explain the wide range of data he had studied. In addition to investigating mediums like Eusapia, he also familiarized himself with the literature on shamans of so-called "primitive" tribes. Later, he studied poltergeist cases such as the one just described. At first, he accepted the "facts" of paranormal phenomena, that is, that the events reported were quite real, but he rejected the idea that spirits or entities were involved. He could easily accept the idea that certain persons, particularly hysterics, were able to focus and transmit energy into a measurable force. This was related to what A. R. G. Owen called the superabundant energy hypothesis. Since it resembled a kind of magnetic field, it might also be related to Rupert Sheldrake's notion of morphic fields, a kind of energy emanating from living creatures. However, Lombroso gradually became convinced that psychic energy transmission, which came to be called psychokinesis, simply did not cover all of the data. It could not account for the reported communications with the dead that some mediums were able to achieve.

As Brian Inglis suggested, the focused way in which psychokinesis operated in the seance room or during poltergeist outbreaks was difficult to square with some impersonal force. In his book, *After Death, What?*, Lombroso finally concluded that "natural" explanations of paranormal events were absurd. He recalled a situation involving a skeptical investigator named Morselli who was horrified when Eusapia had actually materialized his own mother. Eusapia topped this by materializing the loathed dead wife of another investigator who immediately recognized his wife's Genoese dialect, of which Eusapia was ignorant. Spirits or discarnate entities do exist, Lombroso concluded, and they draw their energy from certain people—the medium at the seance or the agent at the poltergeist outbreak.

CHAPTER 8

Two Cases of Electronic Poltergeists

AS WE HAVE SEEN, THE TRADITIONAL POLTERGEIST is a playful creature who pops bottles, throws rocks and household articles, causes objects to disappear and reappear, sets fires, and makes all kinds of strange noises. The development of technology in modern times has brought with it a new kind of poltergeist—one who takes delight in interfering with electronic devices such as telephones, electric typewriters, lighting fixtures, and computers. While the vast majority of electronic malfunctions can be blamed on faulty equipment and human error, several well-documented cases have defied rational explanations. Two cases are particularly worthy of attention. The first takes us to a small town in Germany and the second to Hollywood, California. These cases are interesting not only in their own right but for their theoretical implications. Later, we will consider the idea put forward by some researchers that they be considered "proto-poltergeists," but first let's look at the actual cases.

The Rosenheim Case

The Rosenheim case of 1967 is probably the most celebrated case of an electronic poltergeist. The action took place in a law office in the city of Rosenheim, in the German state of Bavaria. Neon lights attached to the ceiling repeatedly went out, for no apparent reason. Automatic fuses were blown, developing fluid spilled from copying machines, and the telephones began acting up in bizarre ways. The local power company was called in to check on these puzzling events. The power lines were examined by technicians, and an emergency power supply was installed. This emergency unit promptly began to go wild, and other disturbances continued without let-up. The local experts admitted they could not come up with an explanation for these events. The media picked up the story and it was widely discussed by those interested in the paranormal as well as by the general public.

Dr. Hans Bender, associated with the Institute for the Study of Border Areas of Psychology in Freiburg, Germany, was called in to investigate. A leading authority on poltergeist phenomena, Dr. Bender traced the events to Annemarie S., a nineteen-year-old employee. The abnormal events took place only during office hours and when Annemarie was present. In a later symposium on psychokinesis, Bender reported, "When this young girl walked through the hall, the lamps behind her began to swing, light fixtures began to explode, and the fragments flew towards her. In addition, the number of phenomena decreased with increasing distance from Miss S. The case began to show an unmistakable similarity to the so-called 'poltergeist' appearances that we have investigated previously, especially in that the 'agent' was an adolescent."

Bender found that his electronic equipment registered large deflections in the power supply that sometimes coincided with the abnormal events. With a video recorder, Bender's team was able to film and record the swinging of lamps and noises of unknown origin. Initially, they were not able to record a new phenomenon: pictures on the wall suddenly rotated by themselves. In a few cases, the pictures rotated a full 360 degrees around their hooks or fell off the wall. A later attempt by another investigator to record a picture rotation of 320 degrees was successful.

With the cooperation of the telephone company, Bender investigated the telephone disturbances. A test apparatus showed that the time announcement number (0119) was often dialed four or five times a minute. On some days, the number was dialed fifty times consecutively. The employees flatly denied that anyone in the office had made these calls. One observer signed a written statement to the effect that, during a certain time period, no worker had used the phone. Yet, during the same time period, the automatic conversation control registered four dialings of Munich telephone numbers, each consisting of nine digits. It is difficult to understand how a surge of energy could account for these calls since they involved an influence applied to certain springs at specific time intervals. Bender believed that an intelligence with technical knowledge was needed to make such calls.

Two technical experts (one from the Max Planck Institute, the other from the Technical University at Munich) conducted a series of physical measurements in the office during

December 1967. They fitted a voltage magnifier to the line recorder of the power station in order to record the voltage. During one period of an hour and eighteen minutes, the recorder registered about fifteen strong deflections at irregular intervals. Simultaneously, there were loud bangs like those produced by discharging spark plugs but not for every deflection. The experts next set up equipment to record the electric potential and the magnetic field near the recorder and also the sound amplitudes in the office. Their investigation ruled out a number of rational explanations such as electrostatic charging, external static magnetic fields, loose contacts in the electronic amplifier system, and manual intervention. "Accordingly," they stated, "we had to admit that deflections occurred in the recorder, although we had systematically eliminated or checked every conceivable physical cause and made detailed tests to see whether the electrical equipment was functioning properly."

These experts were also unable to explain the other mysterious events taking place in the office. For example, it seemed impossible to explain how light bulbs burst when the light was not turned on and the filaments were still intact. It was equally puzzling that fuses blew when there had been no rise in the current. It seemed to them that the phenomena, including the telephone incidents, were not purely electrodynamic effects. It is quite remarkable that these technical experts reached the same conclusion as parapsychologist Bender—that the events defied scientific explanation. All investigators agreed that some of the events appeared to be controlled by intelligent forces.

The effects at this site came to an end when Annemarie left for another job. However, the poltegeist effects followed the girl. For example, her boyfriend reported that whenever they went bowling, the electronic pinsetters went haywire. This is the last report we have about Annmarie. However, a similar, and equally intriguing, case was to develop in Hollywood, California, some years later.

The second case of an electronic poltergeist was described by D. Scott Rogo in his entertaining book, *On the Track of the Poltergeist* (1986). Rogo has probably written more books about the paranormal than any other researcher, but he is by no means an armchair author. He has personally conducted many field investigations of poltergeist and related phenomena. In this particular case, he worked closely with another well-known parapsychologist, Raymond Bayless.

During the summer of 1978, Gladys Gordon, an employee of a huge plastics factory in Hollywood, got in touch with Bayless. She was concerned about a variety of electronic disturbances in the building, such as loud wailing noises coming over the public address system. Sometimes the call buttons on her phone would light up in rapid, nonsensical fashion. Up to this point, the events had not been harmful to anyone. Ms. Gordon was concerned, however, because it seemed that the outbreaks took place only when she was present—an obvious parallel to the Rosenheim case.

On July 21, both investigators rushed to the plant in response to a phone call from Ms. Gordon. The electronic disturbances had been more intense than usual. Awful noises had been emanating from the plant's loudspeaker. There was a growing suspicion on the part of the other employees that Ms. Gordon was in some way responsible for the outbursts—a situation that was very distressing to Ms. Gordon. At one point during the day, she had left the building for a few minutes, causing an immediate return to normal conditions.

The investigators learned that the plant had a history of problems due to the fact that it emitted intense radio waves. Even though the equipment was now heavily shielded, it continued to put out a high level of emissions. These radio waves were so strong that they could make a tape recorder malfunction. Ms. Gordon and other employees claimed that they could feel the waves. The present outbreak of incidents dating from May of that year was not the first. Similar disturbances had been reported at various times in the past—some of which were associated not with Ms. Gordon but with a previous female employee. This employee's telephone system continually malfunctioned until new equipment was installed. During one previous outbreak of disturbances, a communications expert had been called in to investigate. He recommended the installation of new equipment in a part of the plant reporting disturbances. Unfortunately, the new equipment began to malfunction just as badly as the old. It was the failure of communications experts to solve the problem that led Ms. Gordon to call for the help of parapsychologists.

Ms. Gordon's office was made of dry-wall partitioning and contained some plants, a metal desk, electric typewriter, phone, and file cabinets. As she spoke to the two parapsychologists, the paging speaker outside the office began to sound a high-pitched squeal. The same sound was coming from the other speakers in the plant. Ms. Gordon now predicted to the investigators that her phone would begin to act up, and it obliged by lighting its call buttons in an apparently random manner. Ms. Gordon picked up the receiver and handed it to Raymond who, in turn, gave it to the other investigator. They all heard the same noises over the phone that were coming over the loudspeaker system. Yet, the phone and loudspeaker systems were completely separate systems; one should not have influenced the other.

There was a brief lull in the action, followed by another outbreak with the paging system and telephone repeating their previous performance. In this second eruption, the loudspeakers and phones were no longer in complete synchrony. Sometimes sounds would come over the loudspeaker that were not heard on the telephone. Bayless observed that a small electronic clock on the desk was running smoothly. It was also apparent that a compass Bayliss had brought along was not influenced by the electronic activity. Obviously, the disruptions were selective and did not influence all of the electromagnetic devices on the site.

The investigation came to an end some time later when the plant directors decided they did not want outside investigators at the plant. It was known that the disturbances continued into 1979, and that Ms. Gordon was having similar problems with her home and car radios.

In his report of the case, which appeared in *Theta* during 1980, Bayless suggested that the two young women were acting as detectors who were able to modulate radio waves into a form that could be picked up by electronic equipment. There seemed little doubt that the events originated in quite real radio waves. Bayless concluded that the case should be regarded as a "proto-poltergeist" disturbance since it was closely allied to normal physical phenomena. The present authors find the case fascinating because it shows that some individuals have a heightened sensitivity to electronic waves, and are able to transmit or project these waves to the outer environment.

Dr. Scott Rogo believed that there was an important psychological component to the case. During interviews, Ms.

Gordon admitted that she was under personal stress on the job because of her relationship with her boss. She revealed that the electronic disturbances were worse when she felt herself to be especially tense. As Rogo indicates, this suggests a linkage between this case and the more common family-disturbance poltergeist case. He concluded that Ms. Gordon's subconscious mind played a role in causing the paranormal events. If the cause were merely the radio waves, he reasoned, the outbreaks should have been more random, rather than so closely related to her personal problems.

These two famous cases of electronic poltergeists seem to involve the same kind of events reported by Pauline Shaw of Cheshire, England. A brief article about her by Rick Boling appeared in the November 1988 issue of *Omni*. Boling dubbed her the "electric housewife." Pauline has wrecked about $13,000 worth of electric household appliances in the past few years. She is not a destructive person, but is plagued by a condition that causes her body to emit electricity. She was reported to have ruined twenty-five irons, eighteen toasters, ten washing machines, six dryers, twelve TVs, twelve radios, three videocassette recorders, and hundreds of light bulbs.

Physicist Michael Shallis of Oxford, an expert on body electricity, was quoted in Boling's article as saying that Pauline's electric charge can reach 80,000 volts. Compare this to the microwave oven that puts out 700 volts. He ascribes the electricity to an abnormal metabolism of certain foods. The digestion of food products affects the body's electromagnetic fields. Strong electrical fields can build up in the skin particularly if additional static is picked up from the environment.

The electronic cases are among the best documented in the field of parapsychology. There is little doubt that some individuals are able to generate body electricity, although it is not certain how they do this. They may be able to generate electricity within their bodies through internal activities—as Shallis suggests—or they may be able to transform and discharge energy taken in from electrical equipment—as in the Hollywood case. These processes are not well understood at present, but seem well within the range of scientific comprehension. Much more difficult to comprehend are those events that would appear to be willed or motivated by an intelligent force. It is not difficult to believe that an electromagnetic impulse emitted by an individual could disrupt a telephone, but credulity is strained when specific numbers are dialed. In Chapter 13 we will go into some of the theories which have been advanced to explain these events.

CHAPTER 9

Noted American Cases

THE ASSUMPTION THAT POLTERGEISTS ARE HARM-
less is based on the fact that serious injuries are not generally
reported. However, a formidable figure unmistakably appears
in a minority of cases.

The Bell Witch

As Raymond Bayless observed in his book *The Enigma of the
Poltergeist* (1967): "There is a considerable body of evidence
which clearly indicates that the poltergeist can be a savage
and fearful enemy, possessing grim and mysterious powers."
In the case of the Bell witch, the chief victim was mercilessly
tormented until he died. Paranormal cases in which events are
attributed to witches include some having most destructive
effects.

Before going into the details of this case, a word on the relationship between witchcraft and poltergeists is in order. Poltergeist events were reported long before anti-witchcraft mania reached its height in the late 1600s, and these events continue to be reported to the present day. However, during that period when witches were persecuted, it was often assumed that mysterious events were due to satanic forces. People thought that witches or wizards were able to persecute certain individuals or cause paranormal events to take place. The belief in witchcraft complicates the study of poltergeist cases during this period; it is difficult to disentangle possibly genuine poltergeist effects from imaginary witchcraft phenomena. One difference was pointed out by Bayless: poltergeist events are generally spontaneous in nature, while witchcraft involves deliberate techniques for producing the desired effects, presumably planned and directed by the witch.

In 1846, Richard Bell, who was seven when the witch first appeared, documented the case in a book, and M. W. Ingram provided a more detailed description of the events in a later book, published in 1894.

An interpretation of the case from a Freudian point of view was presented by Nandor Fodor in his book, *The Poltergeist Down the Centuries* (1936). Fodor noted that the case of the Bell witch occurred at a time when most Americans no longer believed in witchcraft. The early 1800s were a hiatus in the history of the paranormal. Witchcraft mania had passed and Spiritualism had not yet become a major movement. However, the details of the Bell witch case make it clear that Americans living in isolated rural areas might still attribute mysterious events to witches in 1817. We will discuss Fodor's theory after reviewing those details.

The setting was a farm in Robertson County, Tennessee, in 1817, where John Bell lived with his wife, Lucy, and nine children. Colin Wilson (*The Mammoth Book*) has suggested that poltergeist phenomena always work their way up from small effects to larger ones—from odd noises to flying furniture. In this case, the first disturbances were so minor that they attracted little attention. Knocking and scraping sounds were heard, usually at night, but these caused no great alarm even though their source could not be located. Next, there were sounds that might have been made by animals—a dog clawing at the floor, a bird flapping its wings against the ceiling, or two dogs fighting. Since no such animals were actually visible, family members began to investigate. However, when they lit lamps and got out of bed to search the house, the noises stopped. It seemed that the invisible entity became bolder and more aggressive as time went on. Clothes were pulled off the bed, stones were thrown, and chairs were turned upside down. These events were accompanied by the sounds of choking, gulping, and gasping as though someone were being strangled. It gradually became clear that these strange happenings only occurred when twelve-year-old Betsy was present.

These inexplicable events continued relentlessly for months, completely upsetting the previous routine of the household. The noises at night were so intense that family members' sleep was often disturbed. Richard Bell recalled that he was awakened in the middle of the night by something pulling his hair so hard that he thought his scalp would come off. At the same moment, Betsy, on the floor above, also began to scream as something pulled her hair. It appeared that the entity, now called the Bell Witch, could be in two places at the same time.

The attacks of the witch became more malicious and centered on Betsy and her brother. Betsy's hair would stand on end as though yanked by an invisible hand, and she was slapped so hard on her cheek, again by an unseen hand, that her cheek would show red. Visitors to the house were also slapped, as were the other Bell children if they tried to resist when covers were pulled off their beds. When Betsy was sent to live with neighbors, the Bell house became quiet, but she continued to be persecuted by slaps and scratches.

An interesting feature of the case was that the poltergeist's noises gradually assumed the quality of a human voice. At first, it seemed to make whistling noises, which were followed by gasping, whispering sounds. It was next heard to speak in an audible whisper, and make crude remarks. It finally sounded like a normal voice, mixing foul language with phrases from sermons. It developed several different voices. One voice declared that it was a spirit that was once happy but was now unhappy: it threatened to torment John Bell and finally kill him. At one time, the voice claimed to be an Indian whose bones had been scattered and, at another time, identified itself as a witch called Old Kate Batts. Four additional voices made their appearance; these were the family members of the witch who called themselves Blackdog, Mathematics, Cypocryphy, and Jerusalem. The latter had a boy's voice, Blackdog had a harsh, masculine voice, and the other two were feminine and delicate. This foursome was often engaged in drunken revelry. Nandor Fodor speculated that the energy for these voices came from Betsy, who was subject to bouts of fatigue. Sometimes she became short of breath and lost consciousness. The voices ceased when Betsy fainted, leading some to believe that she could throw her voice when awake. Fodor doubted that the girl was a ventriloquist, and suggested that she went into trance states similar to those of a medium.

Much as the witch disliked Betsy, her most vicious attacks were directed at John Bell. Once it found its voice, the witch announced that it would torment "old Jack Bell" for the rest of his life and would kill him in the end. Mr. Bell began to show disturbing physical symptoms such as swelling of his tongue and a stiffness in his jaw. It felt as if someone had pushed a stick inside his mouth so that he had difficulty eating. The tortures became progressively more severe with the passing of time. When Mr. Bell was ill in bed, the witch cursed at him. When outside the house, the witch followed him and pulled off his shoes, and, on occasion, slapped him in the face so hard that he was stopped in his tracks. He began to convulse, and the muscles of his face jerked and twitched.

Incredibly, the persecution of John Bell lasted three years and left him a broken wreck. On December 19, 1820, he lapsed into a deep coma. His son, John, Jr., found a dark bottle, containing a smoky-looking liquid, in the medicine cupboard. The witch boasted that she had given a dose to the elder Bell last night "which fixed him." The doctor was sent for and "tested" the medicine by putting a drop on the cat's tongue. The cat jumped up, whirled about, and promptly died. John Bell died the following day, while the witch shrieked in triumph. This was not the end of the infestation, although the household quieted down considerably. On one occasion, during the early months of the following year, the family heard a great noise in the chimney as though a cannon ball had rolled down it and out into the room. It exploded into a ball of smoke as the witch announced that she would be gone for seven years. And so it was. The witch did reappear as promised seven years later, but the episodes were very innocuous and soon ended for good.

Now to Fodor's theory. Fodor was a Freudian psychiatrist as well as an investigator of the paranormal. It is not surprising, then, to learn that he explained the case in sexual terms. He assumed that poltergeists tend to use the energies of a girl or boy who has just reached puberty. Certainly, this coincides with the fact that twelve-year-old Betsy was the original focal point of the disturbances. As is already obvious to the reader, many cases of poltergeist disturbances center on pubescent and adolescent youngsters. In the case of the Bell Witch, Fodor argued, Betsy hated her father because of a presumed incestuous attack on her. Her repressed rage expressed itself in the form of "recurrent spontaneous psychokinesis." The father, in turn, felt intense guilt over his supposed incestuous urges, and punished himself by means of a wide range of symptoms. To support the theory, Fodor cited an occasion when Bell went to dinner with neighbors, but was unable to speak all night. On the next day, he returned to the neighbor's house and explained that his tongue had become immobilized on the previous evening. His mouth felt as though it was filled with fungus. Fodor took this complaint as a symptom of unconscious self-aggression.

In *The Mammoth Book of the Supernatural*, well-known writer Colin Wilson disputed Fodor's theory. He wondered why the poltergeist took such a long, circuitous route to punish Mr. Bell when it could have stated publicly that he had committed incest. This would have been severe punishment indeed. Nor does Fodor's theory square with the fact that Betsy herself was treated badly at first. Wilson also wondered why the witch returned to the house years later when Betsy had married and left home.

Fodor proposed that the poltergeist, the witch in this case, is a "fragment of a living personality that has broken free in some mysterious way of some of the three-dimensional limitations of the mind of the main personality." As Wilson pointed out, "this leaves us exactly where we were before—in complete ignorance of how the split personality performs its paranormal feats."

Since we devoted an entire chapter to the various theories that explain the poltergeist, we will not go into great detail here. However, this chapter would be incomplete without reviewing Wilson's ideas about what *did* cause the events at the Bell farmstead. It should be pointed out that few investigators of the paranormal will publicly admit that they believe in spirits such as the Bell Witch. They would probably interpret the early events as being due to the capacity of strong energy fields surrounding the nine children in the family. The energy became strong enough to influence physical objects. These apparently inexplicable events acted to influence the imaginations of various members of the household, producing physical symptoms of a hysterical nature and hallucinatory effects in others. Many of the more dramatic effects would be ascribed to psychological factors.

At one time, Wilson might have accepted this interpretation but no longer. Based in part on his reading of *The Spirit's Book* by Allan Kardec, Wilson now publicly supports the view that most poltergeists are independent spirits. Kardec, whose book appeared in 1856, was one of the founding members of the French spiritualist movement. Kardec maintained that poltergeists are one of several types of spirit. In particular, they are low spirits, trapped in materiality, who enjoy mischief, evil, and dirty tricks. The haunting of the Bell household, stated Wilson, was the work of not one, but a group, of rowdy spirits of no particular intelligence: "the other-worldly equivalent of a cageful of monkeys." The nine Bell children supplied the energy for the goings-on. Wilson further suggested that the household was not a happy one. In fact, poltergeist events often seem to occur in unhappy homes rather than contented homes. The tension and frustration naturally increase the overall energy level.

The Fox Sisters and the Hydesville Outbreak

The Fox sisters, Kate and Margaret, later joined by a third sister, Leah, are generally considered the pioneers of modern spiritualism. While communication with the dead has been reported throughout human history, Spiritualism as a modern religious movement began with a poltergeist outbreak in the Fox home in Hydesville, New York, during 1848. The manifestations were interpreted by the Fox sisters as communications from persons who had departed this earth. In our chapter on the famous medium, D. D. Home, we discuss some of the reasons for the explosion of interest in Spiritualism during the later half of the nineteenth century.

Home, Eusapia Palladino, Mrs. Piper, and the Fox sisters were some of the best-known mediums, but literally thousands of lesser known practitioners were holding seances in the United States, England, and continental Europe during this period. At first the various leaders of the movement worked independently of one another, but, in 1893, a number of Spiritualist groups banded together to form the National Spiritualist Association. This was essentially a new church, complete with a manual and official prayers and responses. A school was established for the training of mediums and ministers. Although the movement declined after World War I, a number of Spiritualist organizations, with thousands of members, are still active in the United States.

This sequence of historical events began in the rather modest home in Hydesville that was occupied by Mr. and Mrs. Fox and their two young daughters, Margaret and Kate. The house in question had a reputation for strange events prior to December 11, 1847, the day on which the Foxes took tenancy. The previous tenant, who occupied the house for two years, left it because of unexplained noises. The members of the Fox family began to hear noises at night during March of 1848. Raps, knocks, and rattling noises were heard, along with sounds that suggested the moving of furniture. Mrs. Fox described the following events: "On the night of the first disturbance we all got up, lighted a candle and searched the entire house, the noises continuing during the time and being heard near the same place. Although not very loud, it produced a jar of the bedsteads and chairs that could be felt when we were in bed. It was a tremulous motion, more than a sudden jar. We could feel the jar when standing on the floor. It continued on this night until we slept. … On March 30 we were disturbed all night. The noises could be heard in all parts of the house. My husband stationed himself outside the door while I stood inside, and the knocks came from the door between us. We heard footsteps in the pantry … and I then concluded that the house must be haunted by some unhappy, restless spirit."

Mrs. Fox reported that on Friday, March 31, the family members were so exhausted that they decided to retire early and not permit themselves to be disturbed by noises. Hardly had Mrs. Fox gone to bed when the noises started again. "The children," she went on, "who slept in the other bed in the room, heard the rappings and tried to make similar sounds by snapping their fingers."

It was by the action of snapping their fingers that the girls first began to communicate with the spirits. What started as a fairly typical poltergeist infestation soon became more complicated. The girls did not qualify as pubescent youngsters, so often the focus of poltergeist happenings, since Margaret was only ten when the outbreak began and Kate, usually called Cathie, was only seven years old. It was the youngest child who first established communication with an invisible entity by asking that it imitate her actions. "Mr. Splitfoot, do as I do," she said, clapping her hands, and the same number of raps were heard immediately. Then Margaret clapped four times, asking the unknown entity to repeat the sounds. When the sounds were repeated, she was afraid to go on with the game. Cathie wondered aloud if someone was celebrating April Fool's day a little early, and was trying to trick them.

Mrs. Fox decided to test the entity by asking it a question that no one but herself would be able to answer. She asked "the noise" to rap the children's ages successively. Without the slightest hesitation, the spirit rapped out the ages of each child, pausing between each to distinguish them. The message concluded with three emphatic raps corresponding to the age of a youngest child that had died.

Mrs. Fox continued communicating with the entity by means of a simple code. For example, she directed it to make two raps if it was a spirit. When this was answered in the affirmative, she continued in this fashion, and soon established that the spirit was a thirty-one-year-old man who had been murdered in the house. He alleged that his remains were buried in the cellar. After finding out more details of his background, Mrs. Fox asked the spirit if he would be willing to communicate while neighbors were present. Receiving a positive response, Mrs. Redfield was called, and she, in turn, sent for Mr. and Mrs. Duesler, who summoned Mr. and Mrs. Hyde, and so on, until the house was filled to overflowing.

The spirit revealed by means of raps that he had been murdered by having his throat cut in the east bedroom about five years earlier. His body was taken through the pantry, down the stairway, and was buried ten feet below the surface of the ground. It was stated that the murderer, whose name was given, could no longer be brought to justice. The communication was witnessed by over 300 people, some of whom remained in the house all night. On Saturday, April 1, they started digging in the cellar but gave up temporarily when they came to water. When digging was resumed in the summer, a plank was discovered at five feet, and below that a layer of charcoal and lime was found. Finally, the workers found hair and bones that were pronounced by experts to belong to a human skeleton. It was not until 1904, fifty-six years later, that the rest of the skeleton was found. Excavations of the house by the current owner found an almost complete skeleton along with a peddler's tin box. It was surmised that the murderer had first buried the body in the middle of the cellar, but then relocated it so that it would be more difficult to find.

In her sworn statement, dated April 11, 1848, Mrs. Fox declared: "I am not a believer in haunted houses or supernatural appearances. I am very sorry there has been so much excitement about it. It has been a great deal of trouble to us. It was our misfortune to live here at this time; but I am willing and anxious that a true statement be made. I cannot account for the noises; all that I know is that they have been heard repeatedly as I have stated."

In his statement, signed on the same day, Mr. Fox testified to the truth of his wife's statement, adding that, "We have searched every nook and corner in and about the house at different times to ascertain if ... anything or anybody was secreted there that could make the noise and have not been able to find anything which would or could explain the mystery. It has caused a great deal of trouble and anxiety."

In his article on the Fox sisters in the *Encyclopedia of Psychic Science* (19)74, Nandor Fodor stated that Mrs. Fox became increasingly upset by the disturbances, her hair turning white. The phenomena quickly assumed the character of a formal haunting with hideous sounds, the gurgling of a throat, and the dragging of a body across the floor, being heard night after night. "But the raps continued in the house even after they left," Fodor went on, "and one night more than three hundred people conversed with the invisible entity." Kate was sent to live at her brother's house in Auburn while Margaret went to live with her married sister, Leah, in Rochester. The noises followed the girls to their new homes.

A particularly nasty poltergeist outbreak took place in Leah's home. Calvin Brown, a boarder who eventually became Leah's second husband, was observed to be the target of flying objects. Blocks of wood with writing on them were sometimes found scattered about. Leah was to write in 1885 that "pins were stuck into different parts of our persons," and that items of apparel were mysteriously moved from one place to another (quoted by Fodor, 1974, p. 147). It seemed that everything possible was done to annoy them, including loud noises on the roof that sounded like a discharge of artillery. The noises were so loud, continued Leah, that they were heard a mile away. The disturbances continued until a visiting friend revived the idea of trying to communicate with the spirits by using the alphabet. The response to the very first question asked of the spirits was a message announcing the beginning of the Spiritualist Movement. It foretold by means of raps the dawn of a new era, and promised that the good spirits would watch over those who do their duty to God. The manifestations were no longer so noisy or violent, and now included some that were to become standard in Spiritualist seances: the rocking of furniture, the mysterious playing of musical instruments, and psychic touches.

The first meeting of a small band of Spiritualists took place on November 14, 1849, at Corinthian Hall in Rochester. Almost immediately, the movement generated great excitement in the United States, attracting many followers as well as strong detractors. The general public was very much intrigued by the sensational events that were reported to take place during the spiritualist seances and demanded an investigation. One committee studied the Fox sisters and were not able to detect any fraudulent goings-on. A second committee also failed to find any trickery—in fact, it was reported that the observers all heard rapping on the wall and floor when the girls were standing on pillows with their dresses tied tight to their ankles.

Fodor informed us that passions rose so high that on one occasion the girls were nearly lynched. However, neither the hostility of some citizens nor ridicule by some newspapers could stop the growth of the movement. As Harold Steinhour pointed out in *Exploring the Unseen World* (1959), "The thing seemed to be contagious." Sister Leah developed her powers of mediumship almost overnight and was soon joined by many others at Rochester and Auburn. From upstate New York, the movement expanded throughout the United States and then jumped the Atlantic.

Mrs. Fox and her three daughters began giving public demonstrations, presumably at the behest of spirits who told them they should campaign for world enlightenment. During 1850, they went on tour visiting New York City where they met Horace Greeley, editor of the *New York Tribune*. (This was the same man who advised young men to go West.) Greeley reported in the newspaper the findings of a committee of distinguished men: "We devoted what time we could spare from our duties out of three days to this subject, and it would be the basest cowardice not to say that we are convinced beyond a doubt of their perfect integrity and good faith.... Whatever may be the origin or cause of the 'rappings,' the ladies in whose presence they occur do not make them. We tested this thoroughly and to our entire satisfaction" (quoted by Steinour, 1959, p. 37). The "we" included author James Fenimore Cooper, and historian George Bancroft, along with well-known figures from the press, church, and the military.

During these seances only the usual manifestations were reported including raps, the movement of table and chairs, and touches by invisible hands. Some years later, Governor Talmadge of Wisconsin reported the complete levitation of a table with himself on top during a seance with the Foxes. He wrote that the table "was suspended in the air about six inches above the floor." Spirit lights and the apparent materialization of the hands and faces of departed spirits began to occur somewhat later. Leah and Kate were reported to be able to produce complete materializations by 1860–61. During the

1870s, a number of mediums had begun to specialize in materializing spirits.

Relationships between the Fox sisters began to deteriorate. The situation reached a low point when Margaret and Kate, apparently desiring to ruin their elder sister, publicly announced that Spiritualism was a complete fraud. During 1888, Margaret gave a public lecture in New York in which she demonstrated raps on stage, and explained that the effect was achieved by snapping the bones of the ankle and knee. Later that year, Kate came to New York where she also participated in exposure meetings. However, Margaret retracted her statements during the next year, explaining that her great financial difficulties had motivated her to give her demonstrations. These confessions somewhat damaged the cause of spiritualism, but were by no means decisive. By this time, there were a great many practitioners who were regularly demonstrating effects far more dramatic than raps. The Fox sisters all died within a few years after the scandal.

The basic situation of the seance clearly lends itself to fraud: a group of believers sitting around a table in semi-darkness could easily be fooled by a medium with conjuring skills, and there is no doubt that many of the thousands of mediums were indeed frauds. In fact, most of the well-known physical mediums were exposed at one time or another in their careers. Harold Steinour cited Hereward Carrington's estimate that ninety-eight per cent of the phenomena of mediumship are fraudulent. Genuine phenomena are quite rare but as Steinour said "fraud without something genuine that [it] is imitating is also rare." It is quite possible that even mediums who suffered exposure may have occasionally produced genuine effects. After all, they were under pressure to put on an impressive show and may have resorted to trickery to avoid a flop. The pressure was all the greater if they charged an admission fee to the seance or demonstration. As Steinour put it, many mediums were in it only for the quick buck (*Exploring the Unseen World*).

We have used the term *physical* mediums to refer to practitioners who specialized in producing effects that appeared to be impossible from a physical standpoint, such as the levitation of heavy objects. In contrast, other mediums were more inclined to demonstrate *mental* phenomena. These included speaking in a trance as though another personality—sometimes no longer living—were sending a message. Also included under the heading of mental phenomena are automatic writing, that is, writing without paying any conscious attention to the output—sometimes in the handwriting of another person. Seeing visions and hearing voices that others cannot detect are also included. As we explain in our chapter on psychoanalytic interpretations, there is nothing impossible about these sorts of events, since they may represent expressions of the unconscious mind.

Nevertheless, certain of the mental manifestations are very difficult to explain on a rational basis. Joseph McCabe in his book, *Spiritualism* (1920), recounted some impressive performances by Laura Edmonds, the daughter of Judge John Edmonds, who was a respected member of the New York Supreme Court. The judge devoted over two years to the study of Spiritualism, then declared himself a believer. While he claimed no psychic gifts of his own, his daughter developed into a medium with a remarkable talent for music and the gift of tongues. Although she knew only a little French in addition to their native English, during seances she was able to speak in nine or ten different languages with the fluency of a native. McCabe, by no means a convert to Spiritualism, stated that either "the most extreme claim of Spiritualism is true, or the cultivated daughter of a Judge ... resorted to the grossest trickery in order to deceive her father in a matter which he regarded as sacred.... She conversed for an hour in Greek with a Greek.... She talked Polish with Poles. She gave him communications in Spanish (which he knew) from dead Spaniards...." Other young women were also able to give amazing performances. Laura's cousin also acquired the ability to speak in many languages, and Governor Talmadge's thirteen-year-old daughter, who did not know a line of music, performed brilliantly on the piano under control of the spirit of Beethoven. "Either these young ladies got up their lessons in secret," wrote McCabe, "or the claim of Spiritualism is true." As Steinour suggested, it is difficult to imagine Laura Edmonds secretly boning up on ten languages and making trips to the Polish quarter, the Latin quarter, the Hungarian quarter and other places to practice her conversational skills—all for the purpose of amazing papa at some future time.

The story of the Fox sisters illustrates the power of poltergeist events to trigger a very wide range of other paranormal events. Who would have guessed in 1848 that the simple rappings heard in the Fox cottage would lead to the spectacular physical and mental phenomena described in these pages? Or that it would lead to the birth of a new religion with thousands of adherents?

An update on the Fox house was provided by an article, "New York's Land of Dreamers and Doers," in the May 1977 issue of the *National Geographic*. The author, Ethel Starbird, learned that the original Fox house is gone but that a replica has been built in its place. Its owner, seventy-nine-year-old John Drummond, told her that he acted on an inner compulsion which he described as a "calling." An unknown voice told him to recreate the Hydesville house where Margaret and Kate first reported messages from the dead. The author observed another legacy of the Fox sisters in nearby Freeville: Reverend Marion Newbie, at a Spiritualist camp, preached to a small gathering of the faithful that "spirits reach from beyond to communicate with loved ones."

CHAPTER 10

The Seaford Mystery House

THE CASE OF THE SEAFORD, LONG ISLAND, HOUSE begin on Monday, February 3, 1958. At 5:05 P.M., Mr. James M. Herrmann received a call at the Air France office in Manhattan where he was employed as an interline representative. His wife told him that the bottles in the house "are blowing their tops." That afternoon, six bottles, with screw-tops, had opened, fallen over, and spilled in four rooms of their house. The bottles contained various substances, including nail polish remover, peroxide, rubbing alcohol, holy water, liquid starch, and bleach. These events, which at first seemed like part of a practical joke, were the beginning of a case which was to attract national attention from the media. The police, several well-known investigators of the paranormal, and numerous technical experts all became involved.

The Herrmann house was described by a *New York Times* reporter as a carefully kept, white-trimmed ranch-style house which might be "a symbol of orderly suburban life." The forty-two-year-old father lived in apparent harmony with his wife, who was a registered nurse, a thirteen-year-old daughter, and a son, aged twelve. The interior was pleasantly cheerful, with a kitchen, dinette, playroom, and separate bedrooms for the children (Bracker, 1958).

The house was quiet for two days after the first event. The incident that prompted Mr. Herrmann to call the Nassau County Police Department took place on a Sunday morning. He stated that he was standing in the bathroom door as Jimmy was brushing his teeth. All of a sudden, two bottles on top of the vanity table began to move, apparently of their own volition. One bottle moved straight ahead, slowly, while the second spun to the right at a forty-five-degree angle. The first bottle fell into the sink while the second fell to the floor at the same time. on the same day, a shampoo bottle popped its top for no obvious reason.

The Nassau County Police sent Detective John Tozzi to investigate. Some of the more spectacular incidents occurred between February 20 and 25 when he was present in the house. On the evening of the 20th, Detective Tozzi was in the living room writing some notes. He had earlier deliberately placed a full sugar bowl near the corner of the table in the adjoining dinette. All at once, the bowl exploded, showering grains of sugar all over the immediate area. While it was true that Jimmy was seated at the other end of the table, doing homework, the detective was convinced that "no hand had touched the bowl."

An even more remarkable event took place several days later, this time when a reporter from *Newsday* was present in the house. He was alone in the living room at 9 P.M., seated in a chair specially chosen so that he would be able to directly observe Jimmy's darkened room. Suddenly, a ten-inch geographic globe flew across the hall, landing in the living room. Jimmy was sitting up in bed, his legs blanketed. The globe ordinarily occupied a place on a bookcase at the far side of Jimmy's room. In the reporter's opinion, it was "improbable" that the boy had thrown the globe.

On the following day, a statuette of the Virgin Mary flew from a dresser top in the Herrmanns' bedroom to the dressing table. Later that same day, when Jimmy was alone in the downstairs playroom, a portable phonograph at the other side of the room left its stand and flew across the room.

It was inevitable that suspicion fell on Jimmy, since he had been alone in the room when several incidents had taken place, and nearest to some of the displaced articles. Jimmy, an honors student, was considered a bright young man whose head was full of facts about airplanes and rockets. Detective Tozzi, however, believed that it would have been very unlikely for the boy to cause some of the incidents, and impossible for him to have caused others. For example, Jimmy was out of the house when a heavy glass dish fell in the dinette. On another occasion he was on a stairwell when a chest of drawers fell over in another room. On another occasion, the entire family and six guests were together when a dish fell in another room.

During the Spring of 1958, the Seaford house was aswarm with reporters, police, and investigators of all kinds. All kinds of tests were made. A device to test vibrations was installed in the basement but failed to register any movement. A mobile radio receiving station tested the entire frequency of radio waves in the area but found no interference. The chimney was capped to prevent downdraft, again with no results. A technician from Brookhaven National Laboratory showed up with a Y-shaped dowser. He detected energy fields caused by water under the house. He believed that the flow of water could be traced to a recharge basin or sump about a mile away. He went on to suggest that the ice which had coated the sump during the winter had been dislodged by powerful vibrations, possibly from a jet plane, and created a shock wave that was then transmitted by the underground water to the house. This explanation seemed rather far-fetched, but no one was able to come up with a better alternative.

Dr. J. Gaither Pratt and William G. Roll, both then associated with the Parapsychology Laboratory of Duke University, moved into the Seaford house, and began a detailed investigation. A lengthy report of this work was published in the June 1958 issue of *The Journal of Parapsychology*. In their report, they classified sixty-seven puzzling events into categories depending on the type of event, and the location of various observers. Of special interest is a category designated "Disturbances which took place when no one was near." The investigators counted thirteen events which took place when the exact location of persons was known and corroborated by testimony, making it extremely unlikely that anyone could have produced the disturbance without being discovered. For example, on one occasion noises were heard from different rooms, when the entire family was in the living room. On checking, it was found that bottles had spilled in the master bedroom, the bathroom, and the cellar. Once again, the bottles had lost their screw tops. This event is interesting because the noises were heard from three different locations at the same time when the family was together.

A similar event took place when a policeman was with the whole family. Here is the statement from the police record concerning the event:

"When Patrolman Hughes was in the complainant's home all the family was present with him in the living room when noises were heard in the bathroom. When Patrolman Hughes went into the bathroom with the complainant's family he found the medicine and shampoo had again spilled."

Hughes had inspected the bathroom prior to this event and was convinced that everything had been in order. He could not exclude the possibility that someone had turned the bottles over after he had first seen the bathroom, but he could not then account for the noise.

Pratt and Roll were intrigued by the many reported bottle poppings that had taken place in the Herrmann household, and conducted some experiments to find out what would cause a bottle cap to unscrew itself. On the theory that someone in the home had secretly inserted a chemical into the bottles that would create pressure, they placed dry ice (carbon dioxide in the solid state) in containers with screw tops. They found that if the top was loosely screwed on, the pressure easily escaped with a low hissing sound. When the top was screwed on tightly, the pressure increased until the gas forced its way out around the threads without perceptibly loosening the top. The investigators tried various containers under a range of conditions, and could not find any way that the pressure would unscrew caps and cause them to fall off. They experienced only two results—either the gas escaped around the threads, or the bottle exploded. They could not explain the twenty-three cap poppings in the Herrmann household. Five of the bottles were examined in the police laboratory in Mineola. Since there was no foreign matter in the contents, the police couldn't come up with an explanation either.

The Duke investigators considered three types of normal causes to explain the Seaford disturbances: (a) fraud, (b) psychological aberrations, or (c) physical causes. The most likely kind of fraud in this case was childish pranks by the children. Although it was possible that the children could have caused many of the sixty-seven events, there were occurrences "which happened while a third person was actually observing the object that had been disturbed and when the location of James or Lucille was such that apparently neither could have been in bodily contact with this object."

Pratt and Roll wondered if group hallucinations might explain the noises associated with some of the events. They regarded this as an unlikely idea since it required the four members of the family to simultaneously shift into some sort of altered state of consciousness. Furthermore, this theory required that the police and other visitors would have fallen under the same spell. It was concluded that this theory did not merit serious consideration.

The investigators reported that the various physical checks of electrical wires, fuses, underground water, radio frequencies, planes flying overhead, air flow, and plumbing had all failed to provide a satisfactory explanation of the occurrences. They pointed out that these energy sources would act impartially, according to the laws of physics. How then could these forces cause one figurine to fly from a table when similar objects only a few feet away were undisturbed?

Pratt and Roll concluded that the Seaford phenomena resembled the general pattern established in earlier cases, with the disturbances centering on an adolescent. While conceding that they could not offer absolute proof, they believed that the Seaford disturbances might be instances of recurrent spontaneous psychokinesis.

By the end of the summer, Mr. Herrmann announced that he was sick and tired of squads of experts running through the house. A sore point was the request by the Duke investigators that the family members take lie-detector tests. The family refused to take part in these tests because they were afraid that an attempt would be made to implicate the children in the mystery.

The Seaford mystery was dramatized by the Armstrong Circle Theatre in late October of that year—just before Halloween. The actual family members, police, and others were interviewed by Douglas Edwards. This brought to an end the case of the Seaford poltergeist, since no further mysterious events were reported.

Chapter 11

Poltergeists and Psychoanalysis

HOW OFTEN HAVE WE HEARD BIZARRE STORIES OF poltergeists who do their mischief in the presence of teenagers? Do spirits or ghosts single out adolescents for some mysterious, unknown, or perverse reason? According to the Australian parapsychologist, H. J. Irwin (*An Introduction to Parapsychology*, 1989), over seventy per cent of poltergeist "focus agents" are under twenty years of age. A typical case has the following common features:

Jane is a sixteen-year-old whose family members witness objects flying through the air in their Long Island, New York, home—dishes smashing against walls, light bulbs bursting for no discernable reason, the television set mysteriously switching on and off—and all of these unnerving things happen only when Jane is at home.

First, efforts are made to rule out fraud. Of course, a number of adolescents have been caught committing mischief in the eye of a well-hidden camera. Some of their acts of fraud are ingenious in planning, imagination, and creativity. The lengths to which some teenagers will go to con and fool those around them are extraordinary. Why do they do it? What is the motivation for pretending that there is a poltergeist in the house? The need for attention, to be considered "special," or to have your family think of you as "spiritual" or "holy," have all been identified, among other reasons, in these cases of fraud. A particular case of poltergeist activity was investigated by one of this book's co-authors, Dr. Philip Stander, who related the following:

One day I received a call in my office from a former student. She told me of certain friends who had recently moved from Brooklyn to a New Jersey suburb. Shortly after moving into their new home, they claimed that they were being visited by poltergeists. The family invited me, through my student, to come to their home and help them to understand what was happening, and I agreed to go.

I arrived at their home with tape recorder and cameras in tow at about 9.00 P.M. on a Saturday night of the following week, and proceeded to interview each of the eight family members present. I soon discovered that the wife of the home-owner, about fifty-five years of age, and her nineteen-year-old cousin were the only ones who had witnessed the poltergeist activity. No one else had seen or heard anything unusual. The events described occurred on three consecutive nights of the week before I had been called. The mother described how on the first night she was awakened in her bedroom, on the second floor of this two-story colonial home, by noises coming from the kitchen below. She was terrified upon hearing cabinet doors opening and closing. The sounds lasted only for several seconds and, since her husband slept through this disturbance and there were no other sounds that followed, after a short time she went back to sleep. On the second night, her cousin slept over in an adjacent bedroom and, during breakfast on the next day, both confided in each other and other members of the family that during the night they had heard footsteps in the kitchen below and the noise of cabinet doors opening and closing. When all present confirmed that none were responsible because all had slept through the night, the family became concerned that something unnatural was happening. On the third night, the mother was awakened by more of the same, while everyone else slept through it all, including the cousin. This time, the mother heard a woman arguing with what sounded like a young boy.

I was then invited to explore the unfinished attic of their home where, upon ripping up the old floor boards, they had discovered a picture postcard and a toy sailboat. The picture was that of a young mother and her preteen son. The family had left these where they had found them for me to see and examine. Their collective theory was that the postcard depicted the former occupants of the home who, after death, remained as the spirits who were heard arguing and causing the noises.

When I returned from the attic it was a little after midnight, and I was now prepared to witness the phenomena myself. I literally herded everyone into the master bedroom where the mother had originally heard the ghostly sounds, had all the lights turned off except for the hall light directly outside the bedroom door, encouraged everyone to be absolutely quiet, turned on the tape recorder, readied the cameras, and waited for the nightly visitation.

After half an hour and no sound was heard coming from elsewhere in the home, the cousin whispered, "Do you hear that?" Since I hadn't heard a sound, I reminded him not to speak so that I could record any poltergeist activity.

Fifteen minutes later, ignoring my request that no one leave the room, the cousin bolted for the door, which I quickly barred with my body. He whispered that he heard noises coming from the kitchen. Again, I instructed him to remain seated quietly and, after another half hour, with not a sound being heard, I reconvened the group downstairs in the dining room. This time I probed more deeply.

"Why hadn't your husband attended tonight's gathering?"

"He was staying away," his wife responded, "because he didn't believe in any of this."

I asked her, "were you the only one who had heard the voices in the kitchen?"

"Yes."

"How soon after moving to New Jersey did these events begin?"

"Well, when we moved from our old neighborhood in Brooklyn, we left many good friends and family. Out here everyone is a snob. Nobody talks to us, and they all stay to themselves. I am so very lonely and wish we could all move back to Brooklyn."

The cousin then asked me, "Isn't it true that a haunted house is worth more if we go to sell it?"

At that point I was convinced that the "focus/agent" was the mother and, whether or not the poltergeist phenomena were real, once she committed to leaving this "haunted house" and returning to her old neighborhood, nothing preternatural could happen again. And that is precisely the way events subsequently unfolded. The family moved back, I was thanked for having restored the family to its previously blissful state, and another case went into the file cabinet marked with a great big question mark.

The point of the story is that psychological forces often play a major role in creating real or imagined poltergeist activity. Sigmund Freud was first introduced to poltergeist phenomena by his colleague Carl Jung. Early in his career, Freud's skepticism about psychical research, or parapsychology, gradually turned to acceptance and belief. From 1911 on, as Raymond Van Over's research revealed (*Psychology and Extrasensory Perception*, 1972), Freud was a member of the *British Society for Psychical Research*. In an often-cited letter of July 24, 1921, to Hereward Carrington, Freud wrote, "I do not belong with those who reject in advance the study of so-called occult phenomena as being unscientific, or unworthy, or harmful. If I were at the beginning of my scientific career, instead of at the end of it as I am now, I might perhaps choose no other field of study— in spite of all its difficulties!" In that same year, Freud wrote his "Psychoanalysis and Telepathy" (Van Over, 1972), reporting actual case studies of apparent telepathic communication. It is interesting to note that this paper was not published until after his death in 1941. When we read some of the dramatic statements that Freud made, and consider the hostility toward interest in psychic phenomena by most of the scientific community of that time, it is no wonder that Freud decided against publishing his views and findings. It was difficult enough for him to win acceptance for his psychological theories and psychoanalysis. Consider how radical the following would have been perceived to be by Freud's colleagues:

"We must ... at least touch on the question whether real roots of superstition should be altogether denied, whether they are really omens, prophetic dreams, telepathic experiences, manifestations of supernatural forces, and the like. I am now far from willing to repudiate without further ado all these phenomena, concerning which we possess so many minute observations even from men of intellectual prominence, and which should certainly form a basis for further investigation. We may even hope that some of these observations will be explained by our nascent knowledge of the unconscious psychic process, without necessitating radical changes in our present outlook. If still other phenomena, as, for example, those maintained by the spiritualists, should be proven, we should then consider the modification of our 'laws' as demanded by the new experience...."

Only a handful of other scientists of the time believed, as Freud did, that psychic phenomena should be studied scientifically by scientists using traditional scientific method. In 1994, the correspondence between Sigmund Freud and Sandor Ferenczi, the Hungarian neurologist and contributor to psychoanalytic theory, was published by Eva Brabant (*The Correspondence of Sigmund Freud and Sandor Ferenczi*, 1994). These letters (483 in this collection of some 1,236 letters written over twenty-five years) included their secret excursions into the paranormal. In one letter of 1909, Ferenczi wrote of his visit to the medium, "Frau Seidler," who, he believed, had read his mind and thoughts about Freud. Freud wrote back, "I have now overcome the shock, and am confronting the matter just like any other.... In the meantime, let us keep absolute silence with regard to it."

Another letter from Freud, coming one year later: "Quickly, a piece of news ... which brings strong evidence for thought transference. That will certainly be *your* great discovery. So listen. In Munich there is a court astrologer, a woman.... One of my patients ... had his future foretold by her. He gave her the birthday of his brother-in-law ... and she thereupon produced not a bad description of him!"

In 1913, a seance was held in Freud's house "in the presence of ... my children." And so we see that the interest intensified and the experiments continued in telepathy and precognition, but it was in his relationship with Jung that Freud came face to face with poltergeist phenomena. In the remarkable correspondence between Freud and Jung, Jung revealed his belief in both spirits and poltergeists.

In his book, *Freud, Jung, and Occultism* (1971), Psychoanalyst Nandor Fodor informs us that Jung's doctoral dissertation dealt with the psychological aspects of occult phenomena. In this early work, Jung concluded that "... mediumistic development represents attempts at character development in a novel form ..." That is, when an individual is in a mediumistic trance, he or she is open to material from the unconscious mind. In this view, automatic writing and similar manifestations are to some extent products of the unconscious. These expressions of the unconscious contribute to the individual's personality development in somewhat the same way as dream images.

Fodor also revealed that in a lecture given on July 4, 1919, on "The Psychological Foundations of a Belief in Spirits," Jung applied his theory specifically to the poltergeist phenomena witnessed when mediums conducted seances, and stated that "spirits were unconscious, autonomous complexes that appear as projections." To the question, who or what was projecting this energy to create poltergeists, Jung responded that it was the living medium. These poltergeists were the "exteriorization of unconscious complexes."

While in his 1919 lecture Jung appeared to be satisfied that poltergeists emanate from a living person, after attending a seance in 1925, at the home of Dr. Rudolph Bernouilly in Zurich, he did not feel that all poltergeists could be explained as psychokinetic energy from the living. What he had observed at this seance was baffling. Jung observed a variety of psychokinetic phenomena, as well as the materialization of human limbs. Following the seance, Jung was no longer so certain of his earlier conclusion and "that an exclusively psychological approach cannot do justice to the phenomena in question." However, he continued to believe that, for the most part, poltergeist phenomena had their origin in the unconscious mind of the living.

Over time, Jung extended his views on poltergeist phenomena to embrace the belief that everyone had the potential to create such psychokinetic effects with mind energy. Individuals who produce such phenomena, or agents, as parapsychologists have come to call them, can be aware or unaware, conscious or unconscious, of the fact that they are producing these poltergeists. When psychokinesis, or PK, is projected to cause things to break or fly or go bump in the night on a recurring basis, it is called Recurrent Spontaneous Psychokinesis, or RSPK (see page 3).

What is the psychological explanation for such powerful PK energy leaving the mind or body? One theory discussed by H. J. Irwin (*An Introduction to Parapsychology*) is that a person in a state of considerable psychological upset, conflict, and tension, will release the pent-up energy which, in turn, will randomly knock over objects, break, or levitate them. When utilizing the RSPK theory to explain such ghostly phenomena, the assumptions are that poltergeist experiences reflect profound psychological conflict and that they employ a psychokinetic mechanism.

Nandor Fodor, a psychoanalytic parapsychologist, was greatly influenced by Jung and became a staunch supporter of the "subconscious psychokinesis theory" of poltergeists. In his article, "The Poltergeist—Psychoanalyzed" (Fodor, 1948, p. 198), in the *Psychiatric Quarterly*, Fodor argued that, if spirits were not involved and the origin of the bizarre physical phenomena was psychological, then "psychological therapy can effectively ... 'cure' disturbances of such a ghostly character." By correctly identifying the source of the disturbance, an avenue is thereby opened to potentially solve the problem. As Director of Research at the International Institute for Psychical Research in London from 1934 to 1938, Fodor concluded his investigations with the belief that poltergeist manifestations were real, and that the greater number were "manifestations of major mental disorder of schizophrenic, though temporary, character, not the product of anything supernatural."

In his book, *On the Trail of the Poltergeist* (1959), Fodor even extended his psychological premises to include cases of proven, blatant fraud. For example, after S. W., the schoolgirl about whose mediumistic phenomena Jung wrote his doctoral thesis, was eventually revealed to be a fraud, Fodor argued that his premises could be applied; behind even a patently fraudulent poltergeist manifestation was a troubled mind. He urged that psychical researchers spend time on cases of deliberate fraud and not abandon the deceiver because the mental processes that precede or accompany such fraud must be a signal from the unconscious of trouble below and that this "traumatic drive" is the key to the real meaning of the phenomena.

Most of us condemn the con artist who consciously preys on the innocent to cheat them out of money, property or belongings. But Fodor is addressing another kind of fraud where there doesn't seem to be any gain to be made except for the attention received. He reasoned that the fraudulent act itself is to be viewed as a call for help and as evidence of psychological trouble. The appropriate response, then, is to offer psychotherapy in order to get to the source of the problem and, theoretically, put an end to the poltergeist activity.

In relating "The Haunting of Thornton Heath," Fodor revealed that the poltergeist phenomena and the haunting at Thornton Heath had as its focal point a Mrs. Forbes. When it was discovered that Mrs. Forbes was deceiving everyone and that the haunting was fraudulent, Fodor, rather than abandoning the case, began his own investigation. He was intent on exploring the psychological implications of the fraud and discovered that Mrs. Forbes, some nine years earlier, had suffered from hysterical blindness. It was demonstrated that her blindness had no physical cause; there was no damage to the eye, or to the optic nerve, or to the visual cortex of the brain. Her blindness had no physiological cause, but rather was psychogenic, the result of profound and sustained internal conflict and the powerful influence of her unconscious over her conscious self. At the time of the reported haunting, Fodor observed Mrs. Forbes to be neurotic, with a good deal of disorganization in her psyche. She heard voices that indicated a dissociation of her personality. "Dissociation brings in its wake a good deal of cunning and an ability for self-expression both on a conscious and on an unconscious level. For this

reason, fraudulent phenomena should be as carefully recorded as genuine ones. If they disclose abnormal traits, they may
help to bring about an understanding of the supernormal,
since they well up from the same fount." Fodor was able to
conclude, in the previously cited book, that after learning of
her life history and observing her disorganized mental activity, the reported poltergeist was really a construct of Mrs.
Forbes' unconscious self.

In his investigation of yet another case, reported in the
Psychiatric Quarterly, Fodor uncovered real, physical,
observable poltergeist phenomena in a 300-year-old cottage
in Chelsea, London. From his observations of Miss Whalen (a
pseudonym) who owned the cottage and around whom things
went bump in the night and day, Fodor came to the conclusion
that "she was haunted by her own past; that while she had
been successful in keeping some unhappy memories from
entering into her consciousness, she had failed to keep them
bottled up; that her libido had side-slipped and walked out on
her as a ghost, wasting her vitality in a vain attempt to convey
a message in the same way—as in other cases—a symptom
would." When Miss Whalen undertook an exploration of her
unconscious with Fodor and uncovered what she had been
keeping down and repressing in her unconscious; she came to
better understand the desires and feelings about which she
was in such conflict. With further exploration, she came to
accept the source and reason for her inner turmoil, and in a
short time the physical manifestations and ghostly phenomena stopped.

Both Jung and Fodor generalized that, very often, poltergeist phenomena are brought about by an inner conflict that
the conscious mind is trying to suppress and bury because the

conflict itself is too troubling to face on a conscious level. The energy generated by the inner travail becomes manifest as PK, which they interpret to be a cry for help to alert others to the inner distress. In other words, the poltergeist manifestation is merely a symptom of the troubled person's need for help. Through psychotherapy, the ghosts of one's past can be laid to rest, thereby ending the ghostly, physical manifestations. With inner healing, the outward disturbances will cease.

It is only through a reading of the correspondence between Freud and Jung that we learn that Freud actually witnessed Jung making conscious use of PK. Jung had come to believe that everyone possessed the ability to use PK and that the energy was usually projected outward unconsciously. Often, those who were the focus of poltergeist activity were unaware that they, themselves, were causing the activity. The challenge for Jung was to gain conscious control of PK so that, by an act of will, an object could be moved or levitated.

So unsettling was the experience of witnessing Jung using his PK to move objects that, after acknowledging in one letter that he actually saw Jung move objects psychokinetically, in a subsequent letter Freud back-pedaled. Freud could not believe his eyes and now suggested that it was perhaps Jung's use of suggestion that caused him to see what may not have taken place. This kind of denial has often been expressed by those who see things that, if accepted by them as real, would cause a reevaluation of their beliefs about what is possible in this world. After spending a lifetime in denial about things paranormal, it is very difficult for some people to admit that they have been in lifelong error; it is very troubling to have to face the challenge of radically changing one's view of reality and human nature.

Imagine how frightening unconscious PK manifestations are to people who have come to believe in a simple, less mysterious world. Imagine how frightening RSPK is to teenagers who have led relatively sheltered lives regarding the paranormal when, because of their psychosexual conflicts, search for sexual identity, and unconscious repression of their socially unacceptable sexual desires, PK energy explosively and unconsciously leaves their body to do random havoc to material objects in its path. In part, this book is written to allay such fears and reveal how common the poltergeist experience is.

Conclusions

While the psychoanalytic view is that poltergeists emanate from the living unconscious as RSPK, the question remains about the existence and role of spirits, disembodied entities or discarnate personalities in such phenomena. In our discussions with the practicing psychic, Donna D'Alessandro, we obtained another perspective. Donna believes that she has actually witnessed both kinds of poltergeist activity. In several cases she had reason to believe that the activity observed was the result of some spirit whose energy was strengthened by that of the living person. Donna's view is that the combined energy from the living and spirit entity results in poltergeist phenomena, and that when the inner turmoil of the living unconscious agent subsides, the RSPK phenomena cease. Especially interesting is how the views of practicing psychics and scientists, including psychologists and psychoanalysts, are converging in the field of parapsychology.

CHAPTER 12

Daniel Dunglas Home

A WORD ABOUT SPIRITUALISM MIGHT HELP TO place the brilliant career of Daniel Dunglas Home in historical perspective.

Spiritualism virtually exploded on the scene during the second half of the nineteenth century. In her biography of Home, *The Shadow and the Light: A Defense of Daniel Dunglas Home, The Medium* (1982), Elizabeth Jenkins suggested that the social movement called spiritualism arose to fill a deep human need. The triumphs of science and industry had provided support for the doctrine of materialism, which held that all events could be explained by the laws of physical or material substance. Darwin, in his *The Origin of the Species* (1964 edition), dealt a sharp blow to religious faith by casting doubt on the idea that God had simultaneously created the creatures of earth. As the tide of religious faith ebbed, the movement called

Spiritualism suddenly appeared as if to provide reassurance that humans do survive death in some form.

The man who was to become the most celebrated medium of his time was born in modest circumstances in Edinburgh, Scotland, in 1833. His mother was a member of the McNeal Highland clan, who were reputed to have second sight. She was regarded as a seer and, presumably, Home inherited his psychic talents from her. The identity of his father is somewhat in doubt. Home was led to believe that his father was the illegitimate son of the tenth Earl of Home.

Consequently, he pronounced his name "Hume" as the earls did. Daniel was adopted by his mother's sister, Mrs. Cook, and at the age of nine emigrated to America with the Cooks. They settled in a small town in Connecticut and were soon followed by his mother, her husband, and their large brood of children.

When Daniel was thirteen, the Cooks moved to Troy, New York, separating Daniel from his boyhood chum, Edwin. This separation triggered the first of his psychic experiences. One night, soon after his arrival in Troy, Daniel saw a gleam of light in his room. "My attention was drawn to the foot of my bed," he later reported, "and there stood my friend, Edwin." He saw the apparition make three circles in the air with his right arm, and then slowly disappear. Daniel could not move or speak for a brief period. Then he rang the bell in his room. When family members hurried to his side, he told them, "I have seen Edwin. He died three days ago."

Two days later a letter arrived, confirming that Edwin had indeed died after a brief illness.

It was not long before Daniel began to experience a full range of poltergeist effects, including loud raps on his bedhead and the strange movement of furniture and objects in his presence. Heavy pieces of furniture would rise into the air, and tables and chairs would rock back and forth or slide wantonly across the floor. These events were very disturbing to his aunt, the household, and, at first, to Daniel himself. In his autobiography, *Incidents of My Life,* Series 1 (1863), he recounted that he was in his room brushing his hair "and in the glass I saw a chair that stood between me and the door, moving slowly towards me. My first feeling was one of intense fear and I looked round to see if there were no escape, but there was the chair, between me and the door, and it still moved towards me as I continued looking at it. When it was within a foot of me, it stopped, whereupon I jumped past it, rushed downstairs, seized my hat in the hall and went out to ponder on this wonderful phenomenon."

Mrs. Cook was so unnerved by the supernatural events surrounding Daniel that despite the affection he had for her, she declared he must leave her house. So it was that Daniel, a rather sickly, sensitive seventeen-year-old went out into the world, armed only with his unusual powers and a gentle, sympathetic personality. Biographer Elizabeth Jenkins described him as lacking "professional education, without a livelihood, without private means, without a home ... passed from family to family, the quest of people who were not only anxious to investigate his psychic powers but felt a strong personal affection for him."

Daniel believed he could communicate with the spirit world by means of deciphering the raps he heard when he recited the alphabet. After her death, his mother communicated to him in this fashion that he was on a glorious mission to console the weeping and do other good deeds. He became a kind of itinerant medium, giving sittings at the homes of the various families who gave him shelter. It was a pattern that was to continue for much of his life. As his fame grew, he was welcomed into the homes of the wealthy and famous people of the world, eventually including the royalty of Europe. William Thackeray, Napoleon III, the Empress Eugenie, Anthony Trollope, Elizabeth Barrett Browning, and Alexandre Dumas were just some of the famous people who were to become his friends and supporters.

His timing was impeccable. He launched his career at a time when spiritualism was something of a craze in America. As we have seen elsewhere in the book, the movement started in 1848 by the two daughters of James and Margaret Fox in Hydesville, New York, spread rapidly in the United States, and was soon gaining adherents in Europe. Seances became a popular entertainment, with people sitting in darkened rooms while a medium established communication with the spirits. Tables levitated, ghostly figures or parts of figures appeared, and all kinds of raps and bangings were heard. It was no wonder that scientists scoffed at the goings-on and wondered at the credulity of the believers.

In contrast to many mediums, Home was never caught in any trickery throughout his lengthy career. He allowed skeptics and scientists to attend his seances. While staying at the home of a wealthy citizen in Springfield, Massachusetts, Home agreed to be investigated by a delegation from Harvard, which included the poet William Cullen Bryant, Professor David Wells, and two other persons less well known. Here are some excerpts from their report: "The undersigned ... very cordially bear testimony to the occurrence of the following facts, which we severally witnessed at the house of Rufus Elmer in Springfield:

"The table was moved in every possible direction, and with great force, when we could not perceive any cause of motion.

"It (the table) was forced against each one of us so powerfully as to move us from our positions—together with the chairs we occupied—in all several feet.

"Mr. Wells and Mr. Edwards took hold of the table in such a manner as to exert their strength to the best advantage, but found the invisible power, exercised in an opposite direction, to be quite equal to their utmost efforts.

"Mr. Wells seated himself on the table, which was rocked for some time with great violence, and at length it poised itself on two legs, and remained in this position for some thirty seconds, when no other person was in contact with it.

"Three persons ... assumed positions on the table at the same time, and while thus seated, the table was moved in various directions.

"Occasionally we were made conscious of ... a powerful shock, which produced a vibratory motion of the floor of the apartment in which we were seated—it seemed like the motion occasioned by distant thunder ... causing the table, chairs, and other inanimate objects, and all of us to tremble in such a manner that the effects were both seen and felt.

"In the whole exhibition, which was far more diversified than the foregoing ... would indicate, we were constrained to admit that there was an almost constant manifestation of some intelligence which seemed, at least, to be independent of the circle.

"In conclusion, we may observe that Mr. D. D. Home frequently urged us to hold his hands and feet. During these occurrences the room was well lighted, the lamp was frequently placed on and under the table, and every possible opportunity was afforded us for the closest inspection, and we admit this one emphatic declaration—*We know that we were not imposed upon nor deceived*" (source: Mrs. Home, 1876).

The last sentence of the report was italicized in the original, emphasizing the absolute conviction of the observers that Home was, indeed, a "modern wonder." In his memoir, *Incidents of My Life, Series One* (1863), Home recalled that "the power was very strong" during his days at Springfield and that he "frequently had seances six or seven times a day. ..." The house "was besieged by visitors," some of whom came from considerable distances to see him. Although not yet twenty years old, he was already something of a celebrity, his fame having been spread by newspaper accounts that appeared in all parts of the country.

In the same year as the Bryant investigation, 1852, Home experienced his first levitation. "I felt no hands supporting me, and since the first time, I have never felt fear," he wrote, "though, should I have fallen from the ceiling of some rooms in which I have been raised, I could not have escaped serious injury." His arms became rigid and drawn above his head as though he were being pulled up by some "unseen power." Hundreds of levitations were reported in subsequent years. In fact, they often occurred during his seances.

Since it is not possible to describe Home's career in great detail in this brief account, we will focus on some of the *manifestations* that often took place during his services. In 1860, Robert Bell wrote an article, "Stranger than Fiction," that appeared in the *Cornhill Magazine* while Thackery was editor. In addition to the movements of furniture that were typical of Home's seance, Bell reported the appearance of a disembodied hand: " Soon after, what seemed to be a large hand came under the table-cover, and with the fingers clustered to a point, raised it between me and the table. Somewhat too eager to satisfy my curiosity, I seized it, *felt it very sensibly, but it went out like air in my grasp. I know of no analogy in connection with the sense of touch by which I could make the nature of that feeling intelligible.* It was as palpable as any soft substance, velvet or pulp; and at the touch it seemed as solid, but pressure reduced it to air." Many others were to report essentially the same experience with these "Spirit hands," as they were called. As one grasped the disembodied hand, it would simply dissolve to nothing. Thackery, who personally had witnessed some of the Home's phenomena, testified to the "good faith and honorable character" of Robert Bell, whom he regarded as a valued friend of twenty-five years' standing.

Bell also described another phenomenon that was repeatedly witnessed at the seances of Mr. Home—the playing of a musical instrument without apparent cause. Bell recounted that the sitters at one seance heard an accordion play from where it lay on the floor. Not only did it play without hands, it was in such a narrow place that it could not be properly extended. The sitters listened "with suspended breath" to the melody which was "wild" with "a wail of the most pathetic sweetness running through it." Bell did not expect his readers to believe this account, thinking it would be discarded as either fraud or some sort of collective hallucination. He was certain that, given the spatial relationships of the room and the packed conditions, there was no room for any piece of machinery that could operate so large an instrument. The speculations of this kind were dismissed from his mind when he himself held up the instrument in one hand, in the open room with full light on it. He was amazed that the music continued: "... the regular action of the accordion going on without any visible agency." He added that during the loud passages, "it became so difficult to hold, in consequence of the extraordinary power with which it was played from below, that I was obliged to grasp the top with both hands." He witnessed the same phenomenon on other occasions when the instrument was held by others. Mrs. Home in her biography, *D. D. Home: His Life and Mission* (1976, originally published in 1888), unearthed a letter written to the *Morning Star* in October 1860 by another witness to the same events. Dr. Gully, who had been present at the seance when the accordion played, testified that he held it himself for a short time "and had good reason to know that it was vehemently pulled at the other end, and not by Mr. Home's toes, as has been wisely surmised; unless that gentleman has legs three yards in length, with toes at the end of them quite as marvelous as any legion of spirits." He regarded the music as comparable to that played by masters of the instrument. The melodies were grand at times, "at other times pathetic, at others distant and long-drawn...." He also heard the instrument play when it was moved to distant parts of the room "yards away from Home and from all of us."

Continuing in his letter to the *Morning Star*, Dr. Gully recounted some curious events that had not been mentioned in Bell's account. One of these involved a then well-known writer, Dr. Robert Chambers, who asked that his father's favorite tune be played on the accordion which was resting on the floor. Almost immediately a familiar Scottish song was played, which Dr. Chambers acknowledged was his father's favorite when he was alive. Dr. Chambers then requested the favorite one of his father's that was not Scottish. Another direct hit was scored by Home when the accordion played

"The Last Rose of Summer." This was one of many experiences with Home that converted Robert Chambers to Spiritualism. It appeared to him that the manifestations were often governed by some intelligence. Although it was possible that Home had picked up the identity of the two songs by some form of thought reading, it seemed more probable to Mr. Chambers that the spirit of his departed father was present at the seance.

On a later occasion, when Chambers was in Scotland and Home in London, Home received a message from a daughter of Dr. Chambers. Shortly thereafter, this same person appeared at a seance in the company of a sister who had died at an early age. A certain phrase was given by the spirit that was to be presented to Dr. Chambers as a token of identity. Chambers replied in a letter that the words given were the last ones spoken by this young sister before she died. Dr. Chambers regarded this communication as quite remarkable. Further communications from this departed sister showed that she seemed very well acquainted with current family matters. Since it was not unusual for spirits to communicate extraordinary information through Home's mediumship, many previously skeptical persons were converted to a belief in spirits by Home. Typically, he described the spirits he saw, and spoke in their words, but upon awakening from his travel he remembered nothing. Many sitters came away from seances with Home convinced that there was no way the medium could have known about certain facts that were brought to light.

It is not surprising that many witnesses to Home's performances were so moved that they wrote about them in detail. Perhaps the most remarkable of these eyewitness accounts was Lord Adare's *Experiences in Spiritualism with Mr. D. D.*

Home (1869, reprinted in 1976). Based on observations of more than seventy seances, it is one of the most dramatic works in the annals of the paranormal. Here is Adare's testimony about a famous seance that took place in the 1860s: "We heard Home go into the next room, heard the window thrown up, and presently Home appeared standing upright outside our window; he opened the window and walked in quite coolly." This action by Home amazed the observers because the windows of this London house were on the third floor, sixty to seventy feet above the ground. Since there was no balcony outside, the three men who observed the performance could not understand how Home could have moved from one large window to another—by any normal means. More was to come. When Home entered the room, he laughed and said, "We are thinking that if a policeman had been passing, and had looked up and seen a man turning round and round along the wall in the air he would have been much astonished." Home asked Adare to shut the window in the original room. When Adare went to shut the window he found it was raised less than a foot. He could not imagine how Home had squeezed through. Home then asked the others to return to the original room and to raise the window just as Adare had found it. Adare's account continues: "... he told me to stand a little distance off; he then went through the open space, head first, quite rapidly, his body being nearly horizontal and apparently rigid. He came in again, feet foremost. ... It was so dark I could not see clearly how he was supported outside. He did not appear to grasp, or rest upon the balustrade, but rather to be swung out and in."

Another witness named Lord Lindsay wrote an independent account of these events which agreed essentially with that of Lord Adare. Lindsay added that at the beginning of the seance he was struck with a premonition of what Home was going to do. He said aloud in response to a question by Adare, "I cannot tell you; it is too horrible. A spirit says that I must tell you. He is going out the window in the other room, and coming in at this window." Of course this is just what was done a few minutes later.

Both witnesses reported that the distance between the windows exceeded seven feet. The projection or ledge outside each window was about nineteen inches deep and suitable to put flowers on. A string course three or four inches wide ran between the windows at the level of the ledge. "I very much doubt whether any skillful rope-dancer would like to attempt a feat of this description," wrote Lindsay, "where the only means of crossing would be a perilous leap."

Mrs. Home pointed out that the skeptic was faced with two alternatives—either to accept the testimony of the eyewitness "or to suppose that Mr. Home chose to attempt, late at night, the impossible feat of walking along a ledge three inches wide, at a height of seventy feet ... and successfully accomplished the impossible." Even this would not explain the second levitation when Home seemed to float out of the window into the empty air beyond.

Various other possible explanations have been proposed for Home's feat. Frank Podmore, writing in 1902, suggested that Home merely crept back past the three sitters in the darkened room and hopped on the window sill. Psychologist Harvey J. Irwin in *An Introduction to Parapsychology* (1989) expressed doubt about Podmore's idea, and was similarly unimpressed by the notion that the sitters hallucinated the event. Irwin informs us that master magician Houdini proposed that Home could have leaped from one window to the next "if he was fit." This idea seems preposterous in the light of Home's sedentary lifestyle and way of working. We have no doubt that the athletic Houdini could have leaped from one window to another with ease, but Home was a weak, tubercular man whose performances never included feats of athleticism. Somewhat more plausible is the idea that Home could have previously installed some ropes or other supports outside the windows to help him. Somehow we doubt that he would take such a risk, even with ropes, and throughout his career he was never discovered using any sort of contraptions to bring about his effects. Once again, we find ourselves without any really convincing scientific explanation of a remarkable Home performance.

Lord Adare, who was heir to a large estate in Ireland, was a sportsman with little original interest in the paranormal. Although he had nothing in common with Home, the two men became close friends. Adare not only recorded other occasions in which Home seemed to float in the air, but reported other marvels. For example, on several occasions Home walked to an open fireplace and put his face down in the midst of the flames without burning a hair of his mustache. Then he would pick up hot coals and carry them about. Sometimes he would hand a hot coal to a guest, who would also become immune to burning. Frank Podmore, a qualified and skeptical investigator of the paranormal, later stated Home's resistance to heat was the most amazing and best attested of the phenomena presented by Home. The witnesses were many, the illumination was adequate, and the evidence abundant.

Crookes, Home, and Psychic Force

While interesting, some of the manifestations produced by Home are not the kind usually found in poltergeist disturbances. We will now focus attention on the psychic force that Home seemed to possess to an extraordinary extent. Perhaps this mysterious force is also possessed, at least temporarily, by some adolescent or pubescent children who become the agents in poltergeist outbreaks.

During March 1871, Home cooperated in a scientific investigation of this force or power. His attitude toward scientific investigation of his gifts was essentially passive. He did not seek it and was not flattered by it, but at the same time he did not refuse it. Once having agreed to this investigation, he imposed no conditions or limitations, and cooperated fully. He appeared to be confident that Mr. W. Crookes, FRS, a distinguished chemist, would be impartial in his research. According to Mrs. Home, the press was jubilant when it learned that Mr. Crookes had agreed to conduct the investigation. There was general agreement that he was highly qualified to do so since he was cool, clear-headed, and thoroughly scientific in his approach. However, when the findings failed to expose Home as a fraud, Crookes became the target of invective by those who formerly praised him.

Crookes attested that he entered the inquiry with no preconceived ideas. In an article titled "Spiritualism Viewed by the Light of Modern Science," he explained how the scientific method might be applied to the phenomena in question. If the spiritualist tells of heavy bodies being lifted in the air without obvious support, the scientist would ask that this same power be demonstrated by moving a delicately poised balance under test conditions. If rooms or houses appear to be shaken by some superhuman means, the "man of science merely asks for a pendulum to be set vibrating when it is in a glass case and supported by solid masonry." In other words, he intended to measure the psychic force by means of precise instruments. In spite of Crook's obvious intent to conduct the study of Home in a scientific fashion, several of his colleagues of the Royal Society simply refused to get involved. Several well-known persons did agree to help Crookes: one was Dr. Huggins, F.R.S., a physicist and astronomer, and Mr. Serjeant Edward Cox, an attorney.

The conditions under which the seances took place were entirely determined by the investigators. Mr. Home was frequently searched before and after seances, and never objected to this procedure. In fact, Home never objected to any of the precautions against trickery that were imposed by the team of researchers. The seances were held in Mr. Crookes' living room under the close observation of Crookes' associates. All of the witnesses were personally selected by Mr. Crookes. There were no darkened cabinets, and the room was fully lighted. In addition, Home's hands and feet were often held in place by the investigators. In short, the precautions against fraud and trickery were unusually stringent.

Although Crookes himself, along with other witnesses, had seen Home levitate, Crookes was not satisfied with eyewitness testimony. He proceeded to construct instruments capable of measuring the degree of anti-gravitational force that Home could apply. He was aware of arguments that Home's effects were due to his capacity to mesmerize his sitters. It could not reasonably be argued, thought Crookes, that Home was also able to mesmerize scientific instruments.

One apparatus designed by Crookes employed a mahogany board three feet long, one end of which was attached to a spring balance and the other resting on a firm table. The board was fitted with a self-registering balance that would record the maximum weight indicated by a pointer. The board was perfectly horizontal with a wooden foot screwed beneath it. The arrangement was like that of a see-saw. If Home were to exert downward muscular pressure on the far end of the board, it would actually cause the other end, near the scale, to rise, this being due to the fulcrum effect.

Home had not been told anything about the apparatus before he was tested. When he placed the tips of his fingers lightly on the extreme end of the board, the other end *descended*, causing an immediate move of the pointer of the balance. The movement was repeated several times. The normal weight of the board was three pounds, but the index showed a weight of six and one-half pounds. Home had exerted an additional pull of three and one-half pounds. Immediately thereafter, the index showed a reading of nine pounds, thus demonstrating a maximum pull of six pounds. The scientists were astounded that Home was able to produce this effect, which was *in opposition* to whatever muscular force he was exerting. Mr. Crookes stood on one foot at the end of the board that Home had been touching, thereby placing the entire weight of his body on this area. The index recorded an additional weight of only one and one-half pounds on the scale, and this only because his foot extended somewhat beyond the fulcrum—which Home's fingers never did. In fact, Home had been sitting in a low easy chair during the test while his hands and feet were closely watched. Crookes was convinced that there was no material way that Home could have achieved the effect observed.

Nevertheless, critics were not completely satisfied with the experiment, suggesting that Home had somehow managed to exert pressure beyond the fulcrum. Mr. Crookes countered by pointing out that four pairs of sharp, suspicious eyes were focused on Home throughout the test. However, in order to completely satisfy the critics, Crookes modified the apparatus in such a way that contact was made through water only. With the new setup, transmission of mechanical energy was not possible. The apparatus was also improved by providing a permanent record of the degree of weight exerted on the scale. Home was again tested, but this time could only place the fingers of his right hand in a vessel containing water. This movement of his fingers in the water could not itself exert any mechanical force on the scale. When he felt a force coming from his right hand, the recording apparatus was started, and the board was seen to descend slowly and to remain down for about ten seconds. It descended a little more before rising to its former height. The maximum pull was equivalent to a direct pull of 5,000 grains. All of this was observed while Home's other hand and feet were being held. Both Huggins and Cox signed statements attesting that Crookes had prepared an accurate account of what took place during these tests. Huggins did not express an opinion as to the *cause* of the phenomena, but Cox made the following statement: "The results appear to me to establish ... that there is a force proceeding from the nerve-system capable of imparting motion and weight to solid bodies within the sphere of its influence.... I venture to suggest that the force be termed Psychic Force."

Originally, Crookes thought that some actual contact between Home and the apparatus was necessary to exhibit the force. Subsequent experiments showed this was not the case.

When Mr. Home was placed at a distance of one foot from the apparatus, the force still produced an increase of weight on the scale, this while his hands and feet were held. On another occasion, when the power was very strong, Home was able to cause a marked increase in weight from a distance of no less than three feet from the apparatus! The maximum increase of weight recorded during this experiment was about one pound, eight ounces, Ttroy weight.

Another experiment tested Home's ability to play an accordion at a distance. Mr. Crookes prepared a cage consisting of a drum-shaped wooden frame with insulated copper wire running around it. The wire strands were firmly netted together, and the cage was adjusted so that there was no room to insert either a hand or foot into the interior. The accordion was a new one never seen by Home before the experiment. First, Home took the accordion between thumb and middle finger at the end opposite to the keys. Before long, a distinct melody was played based on distinct and separate notes, a result that could occur only if the various keys were depressed. Mr. Home then removed his hand from the instrument and placed his hand in the hand of the person sitting next to him. "The instrument," wrote Mr. Crookes, "then continued to play—no person touching it and no hand being near it."

The electrical current from a battery was now passed around the wire of the cage. When both of Home's hands were in full view, the accordion played again. The accordion appeared to be floating about inside the cage with no obvious support.

Crookes submitted papers detailing his study of Home to the Royal Society, which rejected them without any reason being given. He and his associates, Huggins and Cox, were the victims of gross personal attacks by various members of the scientific community. One critic went as far as to exhibit in public a weighing apparatus purported to be a replica of the one Crookes has designed. The critic accused Mr. Crookes of being ignorant of the basic laws of mechanics. Crookes published a protest showing that the "experiment" shown to the public was unrelated to the actual experiment with Home. The critic covered himself by saying he had been misled about the apparatus by his informants.

Mr. Crookes finally published an account of his most significant experiments with Home in the *Quarterly Journal of Science,* July 1871, accompanied by the testimonies of Cox and Huggins. He stated that he was "surprised and pained at the timidity or apathy shown by scientific men in reference to this subject." He expressed regret that he was not able to obtain a full scientific committee to investigate Home. In view of his own experiences, it should not have surprised him that others were reluctant to expose themselves to attack. Both Crookes and Cox continued their investigations of Spiritualism with other mediums, sometimes putting themselves into situations where fraud and imposture were suspected. Crookes subsequently lost some credibility when he became involved romantically with Florence Cook, a medium he was purportedly investigating.

Home became increasingly concerned about the deceit and trickery of a large number of mediums who were exhibiting themselves in Europe and the United States. He began working on a book, *Lights and Shadows of Spiritualism* (1877), that exposed the abuses that were bringing Spiritualism into disrepute. When it appeared in 1877, the book detailed the kind of impostures that would help put the credulous sitter on guard. However, true to his gentle nature, Home did not list the names of those who had been caught cheating. He also criticized the movement of Theosophy which was then actively teaching "The Wisdom of the East" and, in effect, weakening Christianity. It should be kept in mind that Home was a devout Christian. He gently ridiculed the doctrine of reincarnation by pointing out that he had personally met three women who claimed to have been Jezebel in a past life.

Home continued his lifestyle of frequent travels to Russia, Switzerland, France, Italy, and other countries, giving seances everywhere. His wife and some friends were increasingly concerned about the threat to his delicate health of his continued work. On one occasion, he was to be investigated by a scientific committee headed by Professor von Boutlerow of the Academy of Science in St. Petersburg. Although quite ill with tuberculosis, Home insisted on going through with a planned seance. Slight oscillations of a glass-topped table were the only effects observed. Similar failures to produce spectacular effects had sometimes been observed by Crookes when Home was in a physically weak state. Home was again tested by the same Russian scientists on a subsequent visit to St. Petersburg. This time, the results were far more impressive. The investigators repeated the experiments earlier performed by Crookes with somewhat different equipment. A dyna-mometer was arranged in such a way that any pressure exerted by Home's hand would diminish, instead of increase, the tension. Home increased the tension in the dynamometer to 150 pounds from its previous level of 100 pounds—a quite spectacular feat!

In this brief account, we have emphasized those aspects of his work that may have relevance to poltergeist disturbances. From *his* perspective, the most important aspect of his work was the linkage he provided with the spirit world. Home rarely lectured or preached, but attempted to inform others by providing proofs of a nonmaterial world. In this view, a newly departed spirit was sometimes disoriented, and sometimes unable to accept the fact of having left the earth. Gradually this spirit comes to realize that death is not the end but a second birth. According to many communications received by Home, there is no Heaven or Hell, but a luminous place providing opportunities for continued spiritual growth. Some of his ideas of a spirit progressing through higher and higher spheres are similar to those previously expressed by the Seeress of Prevorst. Contemporary psychics sometimes encounter spirits that have lost their way and attempt to influence events on earth. In fact, this is one possible explanation of some poltergeist disturbances.

After a long period of pain and suffering, during which he gradually became an invalid, Daniel Home died in June of 1886. Mrs. Home told friends that he was mainly concerned during his last days with inspiring her with the strength to go on, and reassuring her that he would not be far away after his death. Thus ended the life of one of the most amazing persons in the annals of the supernormal. "His aim," Mrs. Home wrote, "was the propagation of Spiritualism, especially among those who have lost the innate perception of spiritual things" (*D. D. Home*). We have returned to the point made at the beginning of this chapter. Home and the Spiritualist movement attempted to reassure us that death was not the end. He himself faced death with serenity based on a conviction of an afterlife.

CHAPTER 13

The Poltergeist in the Laboratory

FOR THE SCIENTIST, THE PROBLEM OF STUDYING poltergeists is that they occur unexpectedly, and seemingly beyond our control, so that there is little chance of duplicating the strange events in the laboratory. In most instances, the events occur and recur in the vicinity of individuals who seem to attract poltergeists—or to produce them. If such individuals will serve as volunteer subjects in laboratories, then the phenomena can be witnessed under controlled conditions.

Traditionally, scientists have been skeptical of the existence of such bizarre events, but the sheer numbers of reported cases have softened this skepticism. For example, in March 1987, the first news item ever published in the USSR about reported cases of poltergeist activity appeared in the *Moscow News*. Significantly, the article, which was reported by the Foundation for Research on the Nature of Man, ended with a plea for increased scientific investigation of poltergeist phenomena. Since the founding in 1882 of the Society for Psychical Research in London, scientists have been investigating such phenomena. Examining poltergeists under controllable conditions with results that can be repeated and reproduced in any scientific laboratory has proven to be very difficult. During the period from 1932 to 1951, research on a wide range of psychic phenomena was done at Duke University in Durham, North Carolina, by pioneer investigators William McDougall, J. B. Rhine and his wife, Louisa E. Rhine. *The Journal of Parapsychology* was established in 1937, in order to report such investigation and experimentation.

Another milestone in establishing the field of parapsychology as credible and respectable was the acceptance of the Parapsychology Association (founded in 1957) as an affiliate of the prestigious American Association for the Advancement of Science (AAAS) in 1969. Full members of the Parapsychology Association must have earned a graduate degree and made a significant contribution to their field. There is an increasing sense of pride in the field as parapsychology becomes more and more accepted by mainstream scientists working in traditional areas such as biology, physics, and medicine.

Today, scientists in the field of parapsychology are focusing on the kinds of poltergeist that may be created by a living person's own energy. On the face of it, that seems to be an approach more likely to bring results, in contrast to proposals for catching a ghost, or inviting one into the laboratory to show its "stuff" and demonstrate what it is made of, or produce effects such as levitating tables on demand. It is remarkable that so many scientists and reputable physicists have entered the field of parapsychology, but before we review their work, let us examine an extraordinary experiment intended to create a ghost.

In 1976, a privately funded organization of people who wanted to further their knowledge of parapsychology, the Toronto Society for Psychical Research, conducted an experiment to create a poltergeist out of a group of people's collective psychokinetic energy. Some researchers call this Group PK, or PK-by-committee. Step by step, eight individuals who never claimed to be psychic or to have had psychic experiences met once a week, creating the fictitious story of Philip, and then made "Philip" come to life.

As recounted by authors I. M. Owen and M. Sparrow (*Conjuring Up Philip: An Adventure in Psychokinesis*, 1976), here are the essential elements of Philip's fictional biography, which were later filled in and elaborated by the group: Philip, an aristocratic Englishman living in the 1600s, was unhappily married. He subsequently fell in love with a gypsy woman. His wife, in a jealous rage, caused the gypsy's death by accusing her of witchcraft. Heartbroken, Philip killed himself.

After a full year of reviewing the elements of the story, elaborating on the details, producing a picture of Philip, engaging in meditation and then using the method of a Seance Circle as designed by K. J. Batcheldor, Philip was "born." At first, members of the group felt vibrations from the top of the table, and then heard loud rappings. A simple code was created and soon Philip answered questions with one rap for "yes" and two for "no." As the sittings continued, Philip was able to do more, much of it captured in very bright light by television cameras. For example, if a member of the group walked into the room late, the table would rush across the room to the latecomer. On other occasions, lights on a panel would flicker in response to verbal instructions. At times the table would creak and groan as if something were trying to take it apart. Toward the end of the experiment, the group witnessed the table raising three legs off the floor, sometimes sliding about the floor in a random manner, and at other times rocking and jumping as if Philip were being playful. At the end of January 1974, the group made a documentary film, *Philip, the Imaginary Ghost,* which told the story of the experiment and captured the movements of the table and sounds of the raps on film.

After reading this story, you may still question whether a discarnate personality, or ghost, produced the poltergeist phenomena. In coming to grips with this question, it is important to note that, when Philip was asked questions of fact about the 1600s, the time in which he "lived," often his answers were wrong simply because the members of the group didn't know the correct answers. In fact, a lack of knowledge and uncertainty in the group resulted in raps that were hesitant, or loud scratching noises on the bottom of the table. This would lead us to believe that the phenomena were created by group PK and not an independent entity.

There was a case reported in 1876 that is very similar in its implications to the Philip case. In England, a well-known and respected solicitor reported that, one summer, his ten-year-old daughter seemed to be followed by blows and strange noises. When she would sing a happy tune, the raps would become louder and beat in time with the music. Her father developed an alphabet code in order to communicate with whatever was producing the rappings. From decoding the rappings he learned that this was a young boy with the knowledge and intelligence of his daughter, leading him to conclude that contact with the boy was a product of the little girl's psychic ability and imagination.

More recently, William Roll of Durham University reported an experiment with a young boy from Miami, Florida, who, witnesses reported, seemed to cause objects, including glass and china, to fly from shelves around him. In the laboratory, Roll reported that the boy was able to order certain objects to move from shelves. In another demonstration of psychokinesis, Roll cited the case of Virginia Campbell who, on one occasion, willed an apple to come to her from across the room.

Because of the great number of such cases reported, psychokinesis research was begun at Duke University in 1934. The major intention was to see whether scientists could demonstrate a direct effect of the mind on matter under strictly controlled experimental conditions. In 1973, Louisa E. Rhine and Sara R. Feather reported on two experiments, in which they both took part, to try to answer a similar question raised by those who conjured up Philip. Specifically, they wanted to determine whether two subjects trying to influence an object in the same direction would produce a greater effect than one. It should be noted that, in the case of Philip, effects were being produced when as few as four people were present. Rhine and Feather theorized that several people acting together might amplify the PK effect.

In the Rhine/Feather experiment, the targets were dice. When the women tried to get the same target face to come up on rolling dice, they either succeeded very well or missed very badly.

Betty M. Humphrey, in her 1947 experiment, employed a subject who alternated randomly between trying to "help" a subject to make a given face turn up on the dice, or to "hinder" by wishing for a different number. Significant positive scoring was achieved when both tried for the same face, while insignificant results were found when each tried for a different target. Note that the Rhine/Feather study failed to confirm Humphrey's. Subsequently, when Rhine and Feather used a rectangular plexiglass box rotated by an electric motor with baffles on the inside walls, the dice fell twenty-four inches to the other end, thereby assuring ample rotation. This was an improved method over earlier research and, under these new and different conditions, the results were as predicted.

Dice, as targets, were introduced by J. B. Rhine in the earliest experiments in PK and continue to be the targets of choice by most experimenters. One reason is that statistical analysis in such experiments makes it easy to determine the odds of the effect taking place. That is, it is easy to compute if the effects of the experiment can be explained away by probability theory as luck or chance, or if the results are unusual and, therefore, extra-chance. For example, if six dice are placed in a tumbler that is rotating and mixing the dice, when the PK agent tries to make sixes come up on all six dice, the results of this experiment are easy to calculate. In the case of someone who makes sixes come up repeatedly, you do not need a calculator to tell you that what is happening violates the laws of chance and probability theory. It is clear that something unusual is happening, and the parapsychological explanation is that the experimental subject, the person whose PK is being tested, is using PK to control the roll of the dice.

Another kind of PK experiment in which dice are used is called the placement test. Here, the subject is asked to cause rolling dice to fall down a slide on to one part of the floor or the other. Of course, if uninfluenced by PK, the dice will land distributed in a random pattern across the entire floor, but if the subject uses PK to make all the dice land on one side or the other of the marked floor, on demand, the conclusion is that PK has been demonstrated.

Another reason for using dice, in addition to the ease with which we can determine whether the results are chance (luck or coincidence) or extra-chance, is that it takes very little energy to influence small, rolling objects. The fact that the dice are moving means that there is very little friction to overcome. High scores on such tests are considered by scientists to be micro-effects. Generally, parapsychologists accept the existence of micro-PK events, which are the small PK effects that are apparent only when they are repeated thousands of times. To produce macro-effects, however, heavier objects at rest must be moved by PK energy.

In recent experiments, targets other than dice have been used. For example, W. E. Cox conducted a PK experiment in which the subject tried to affect the movement of a pendulum. The subject's task was to try to lengthen or shorten the pendulum's swing. The pendulum was connected to an electric system that recorded its movement and, from the record produced, Cox concluded that the experiment successfully demonstrated the power of PK. Cox has also used such targets as coins, balls, BB slugs, water spray, mercury globules, soap film, air bubbles and electric relays in demonstrating the reality of PK. In a series of six experiments, Bob Brier (currently the Chairman of the Department of Philosophy at C. W. Post College and formerly J. B. Rhine's chief statistician) used two small philodendron plants as targets. Ten subjects were used. Each subject was asked to concentrate on a plant in order to increase activity in it as measured by a polygraph to which it was attached. Brier concluded that PK seemed to be the cause for the increased activity in the plants, and that the results of the pilot tests warranted a full-scale investigation of the possibility that PK affects living tissues.

Since then, a series of experiments have been conducted by independent researchers with the same results. For example, Jean Barry reports on experiments that were conducted in an agronomy laboratory that succeeded in retarding fungus growth with PK energy under strictly controlled conditions.

Such experiments of PK's effect on living organisms suggests that many in the healing professions have correctly surmised that their own bodies may be producing energy that can affect the tissues of their patients. Specifically, the pioneer research on "therapeutic touch," described by Robinson and carried out by Dolores Kreiger, Professor of Nursing at New York University, and by Thelma Moss and others, suggests that PK energy transmitted by health practitioners can "heal" and have measurable, beneficial effects, including speeding up the body's own regenerative abilities.

Another method of determining whether PK can influence another's body is called biofeedback. In experiments conducted by William Braud and Charles Honorton, the target person's physiological activity is monitored by a biofeedback device. As described by Robinson, a subject tries to affect the target person using PK, and the biofeedback device reveals how the subject is doing. Such experiments reveal that one person can affect another's body by PK.

Among the outstanding physicists currently studying micro-PK in the laboratory is Helmut Schmidt, originally with the Boeing Laboratories in Seattle, Washington, then at the Institute for Parapsychology in Durham, and now at the Mind

Science Foundation in San Antonio, Texas. Rogo described Schmidt's contribution to the development of random event generators (REGs) in the 1960s.

The observable part of the REG is a panel of nine lights arranged in a circle of about a foot in diameter. Under normal conditions, when no one is attempting to influence the REG, the lights will light up back and forth randomly. That is, a light on the REG panel will randomly flash on to the left or to the right. The REG's electronic circuitry is connected to a piece of radioactive Strontium 90 which, as it decays, randomly throws off electrons. The lights will blink to the left or right in a random, unpredictable way, because no one can predict when an electron will shoot off. Therefore, in any given time period the light will randomly blink on to the right fifty per cent of the time, and to the left fifty per cent of the time. This effect can be compared to the flipping of a coin which, in a given period of time, will randomly come up heads fifty percent of the time and tails fifty percent of the time; no one can predict precisely when the coin will come up heads or tails.

In Schmidt's REG experiment, the PK testee is told to try to make the lights flash in one general direction. For example, the subject may be told to make the lights blink on to the right so that they appear to move around the circle progressively. As in the case of coin flipping, it is as easy to compute the odds of a given number of lights flashing on to the right after one thousand trials as it is to compute the odds of a coin coming up tails after that many flips. Therefore, if a subject can will the light to blink on beyond chance expectations, then a PK effect is said to have been demonstrated.

Experimenters such as Schmidt, Jahn, and Radin find that using the REG is superior to using dice, because the REG can be connected to a microcomputer so that outcomes are automatically recorded and scored without a chance of human error. In addition, a very great amount of data can be obtained in a relatively short period of time.

Robert George Jahn has emerged, in the 1960s, as one of the most respected researchers of PK in the world. He is dean emeritus of Princeton University's engineering school (after fifteen years of service), a recognized leader in aerospace engineering, and the author of *Physics of Electric Propulsion*, the leading textbook in the field. In 1979, when he switched the focus of his work from NASA to ESP and PK, he surprised a number of colleagues in the scientific community. At that time, Jahn created the Princeton Engineering Anomalies Research (PEAR) lab and continues his PK experiments with a team comprising of an astrophysicist, an electrical engineer, a behavioral psychologist, a developmental psychologist and an experimental psychologist (S. Fishman, "Questions for the Cosmos," in *The New York Times Magazine*, November 26, 1989, p. 54).

The REG, as used by Jahn and his team, has a bright red digital readout. The volunteer subject is seated in front of the machine and is asked to think "high" or think "low" or, in the language of coin flipping, to think of heads or tails coming up. Statistical analysis of the results occurring by chance are one in five thousand. The majority of volunteers achieved extra chance scores and, by inference, Jahn suggested that the majority of earth's population could perform similarly. The suggestion, of course, is that to be human is to possess PK ability.

In the laboratory's main room is a device the staff calls "the pinball machine" which took five years to complete. The device, formally named the "random mechanical cascade," has 9,000 black, polystyrene marbles (each three-quarters of an inch in diameter) atop a six-foot wide, ten-foot high construction, which are dropped through 330 pegs, finally landing in 19 bins. Since, under normal conditions, more balls fall in the center bins than in the outer bins, the distribution of balls looks like a bell-shaped curve. The volunteer facing the device is asked to make more balls fall into the bins to the right or to the left. Results of the 3,393 runs, or experiments, reported at the time of publication, were that there was only a one-in-20,000 probability of such high scores happening by chance.

According to S. Fishman's article, "Questions for the Cosmos," in *The New York Times* (November 26, 1989), Jahn plans a number of experiments for the future: to use PK to change the temperature of the water in a fish tank, to alter the glow of a long, wide vacuum tube that lights up when electricity is sent through it, and to lift (or levitate) a weight suspended from a bar. Future publications of his PK experiments should prove to be of great interest.

Gertrude Schmeidler, a psychologist long affiliated with the City College of the City University of New York, and now professor emeritus, engaged in ESP research for decades and is best known for her research into the personality characteristics of both high and low scores on tests of ESP talent. In an experiment, as told by Rogo, she tested psychic Ingo Swann's claim that he could alter the surface temperature of objects using PK. Swann is very well known by researchers of parapsychological phenomena; he has been a volunteer in a wide range of ESP and PK experiments. In this experiment, Schmeidler hooked each of a series of pieces of bakelite and graphite to a sensitive device which continually recorded their temperatures. Swann succeeded in making each piece of material either warmer or cooler by simply willing it. The unexpected outcome, not predicted by Schmeidler, was that when one object altered in temperature, the other objects being monitored altered in the opposite direction, as if heat was transferred from some pieces to raise or lower the temperature of the target piece.

This brings us to the claim that fires have sometimes been caused, spontaneously, by the unconscious direction of PK energy. The literature contains many cases of spontaneous combustion where objects or walls suddenly burst into flame. The theory suggested is that individuals (often adolescents in the vicinity) acting as unconscious agents, send out bursts of PK energy when their psychological state or mood is one of anger, frustration, or emotional disturbance. Such energy may be so intense that it does more than simply raise the temperature of Jahn's experimental fish tank by a few degrees, or slightly raise the temperature of pieces of graphite in Schmeidler's lab. The suggestion is that intense PK energy can raise the temperature of an object to its combustion point.

Some, like Vincent Gaddis (*Mysterious Lights and Fires*), have suggested that PK may also cause an immunity to burning. In his description of firewalking, he cites a number of instances of people in various cultures who have walked on fire and have neither felt pain nor been injured. While it is understandable that firewalkers may feel no pain because they are in a self-induced hypnotic trance or religious ecstacy, which may in fact block the perception of pain, how do we explain the absence of injury or burning of the skin?

In the native religions of tribes or peoples of the Pacific Islands, South America, or India, where firewalking is practiced, the belief is that tribal and ancestral spirits give protection and shield the walker from burning. Of course, if you walk quickly across the hot stones, coals, or wood embers, your feet are not on the fire long enough to be burned. In addition, physicists have discovered the Leidenfrost effect, consisting of a very thin layer of water vapor on the soles of your feet due to sweat or water evaporation which offers protection for a brief period of time. However, how do you explain the absence of burning when the firewalking is slow and deliberate? Some have suggested that PK energy may provide an energy barrier which prevents burning and, for a short time, creates an immunity to burning. Additional research is needed to determine the reality of such a macro-PK effect. Macro-PK, sometimes called "directly observable PK," is easily visible to the unaided eye. Poltergeist phenomena fall into this category and most reports generated are of spontaneous, unexpected, uncontrolled phenomena. Parapsychology laboratories around the world have attempted to bring the suspected agents of such phenomena into the laboratory in order to duplicate the actions of the poltergeist. Ideally, scientists in all realms of investigations hope to be able to fully explain the nature and causes of these events so that they can predict the event before it happens; with the power to predict comes the power to control. In the course of scientific exploration of PK, several individuals have volunteered to come to the laboratory to serve as subjects, claiming that they have pronounced PK ability and can produce macro-PK effects on demand.

In their widely read book, *Psychic Discoveries Behind the Iron Curtain* (1970), Ostrander and Schroeder describe scientific experiments in parapsychology conducted in Soviet Russia, Bulgaria, and Czechoslovakia. The experiment performed in the Soviet Union by Naumov involved a woman who claimed that she had special powers, a Mrs. Mikhailova. Before the experiment began, a full physical exam, including x-rays, was administered by a medical doctor in order to rule out fraud and determine with certainty that no hidden objects or magnets were concealed in her body. In the first of many experiments with her, she held her fingers about six inches over a compass and, after twenty minutes, her pulse rate had increased to 250 beats per minute. Suddenly the compass needle shivered, began to spin counterclockwise, and then the entire compass, plastic case and all, began to whirl. In another experiment, a glass bowl was filled with cigarette smoke and placed upside down in front of her. Then, from a distance, directing her PK, she cut the mass of smoke in half as if it were a solid.

Research in the USSR has continued in great earnest by such respected scientists as Soviet physicist Victor G. Adamenko. Dr. Adamenko, an important member of Moscow's psi research community, left the USSR and is currently living in Greece. Now on the faculty of Crete University, Adamenko is director of the new psychophysics laboratory where he will continue to engage in macro-PK research. As reported in an interview at The Foundation for Research on the Nature of Man (FRNM) in Durham, most of his research is aimed at understanding the macro-PK effects of such remarkable subjects as Nina Kulagina and Alla Vinogradova (L. Vann, Ed., *The FRNM Bulletin,* No. 39, 1988, p. 2).

Kulagina is perhaps the best known of the subjects studied. She is reported to have performed healings, caused objects to levitate, and produce images on photographic materials. In

1968, participants in an international conference on parapsychology in Moscow were shown a film in which Kulagina was
seen moving objects across a table without having any physical contact with them. Soon after, scientists and parapsychologists came to test her. One such scientist, clinical psychologist
Dr. Glen Boles, visited the laboratory along with other scientists from the United States, to witness Kulagina perform in an
experimental setting. In an interview provided exclusively for
this book, Boles revealed that the visiting team literally tore
the room apart in their efforts to rule out fraud. Before, during,
and after Kulagina's demonstration of PK, neither Dr. Boles
nor any of the accompanying scientists, nor any scientist since
has detected even the possibility of trickery.

In his interview at FRNM, Dr. Adamenko revealed that, in
December of 1987, Nina Kulagina won a court case against a
leading Soviet magazine that had published an article describing her PK effects as fraudulent. Testimony at the trial from
Soviet scientists contributed to her victory in court. It is interesting to note that the film of Kulagina moving objects with
PK shown at the 1968 Moscow conference was included in a
science documentary, "The Case of ESP," produced by Nova
for public television in the United States.

Dr. Adamenko has learned enough about the nature of
macro-PK to teach techniques by which anyone can develop this
ability. He teaches students to move small electro-statically
charged objects: to roll, rotate, and slide objects such as
matchsticks, styrofoam cups, or empty plastic or metal cylin-
ders along a plexiglass surface by passing a hand over the
object. Most people can easily learn to induce such effects,
which can be simply explained by electrostatics. However, a
few people demonstrate, after long practice, the ability to

move much heavier objects over more resistant surfaces such as wood. Adamenko claims that his careful measurements indicate that electrostatics and other known energy fields cannot fully account for these effects.

To date, Adamenko's best subject is Alla Vinogradova. Two years into her training, she began to produce macro-PK effects. According to Robinson, sparks have been seen at her fingertips while she is working, yet she can move objects even when she is electrically grounded. Adamenko has thus far learned that, while ultraviolet light emissions and electrostatic fields accompany these effects, they do not account for macro-PK activity (FRNM, 1988).

It is obvious why governments are interested in the military implications and applications of macro-PK. Consider the fact that very little PK energy is needed to interfere with delicate electronic circuitry in today's sophisticated weapons, and very little PK energy is needed to interfere with computers and other industrial devices. Consider how little force is needed to press a button in a factory, a computer, or on a pad that launches a missile. What if the energy is amplified by generating PK by committee or a large group? There is literally no end to the mischief that could be done by poltergeist activity unleashed by a hostile, belligerent nation.

On the other hand, think of the good that could be done by health professionals who use PK to heal and regenerate tissue, or contribute to our knowledge of the mind and body. In the final analysis, psychic forces are neither good nor evil, but merely part of the natural world. Ultimately, we will determine whether these talents are put to moral or immoral uses.

Chapter 14

A Summing Up: Theories of Poltergeists

IF YOU HAVE EVER COME FACE TO FACE WITH SOMEthing bizarre, outside the realm of your ordinary, daily experiences, it can be so shocking that you may come away from it doubting your own sanity. Countless numbers of people have had such experiences. However, it is particularly frustrating to be alone when it happens and there are no eyewitnesses. Even more frustrating is when the experience happens only once in your lifetime, never to be repeated. So many people whom we have talked to, who had the courage to reveal their experiences to us, confess that they never told anyone else of the experience, lest they be thought of as "crazy." Parapsychologists refer to such singular, unexpected events as "spontaneous phenomena." Those events that recur and involve a discarnate entity, usually in the same home or place, are called "hauntings." When the working scientist, or professional parapsychologist, is privy to such an anecdotal report of a haunting or poltergeist activity, the analysis and investigation considers the following hypotheses or theories.

Fraud

The story that the teenage girl tells of the poltergeist seems straightforward enough. She says that, when she returns home from school each day, she usually sits in the overstuffed chair in the living room to watch television. Before long, the telephone receiver on the table to her left comes flying by her, sometimes almost striking her, and if not for the wire to which it is attached, would probably fly off into the next room.

The girl's parents never see it happen directly but, when they are in the room watching TV with her, they will hear her shriek and they turn to see the receiver end its flight on the floor. When these unnerving flights persist and the girl seems to become increasingly agitated, they call for help through the local newspaper whose editor sends a photographer to visit and hopefully catch the event on film.

When the photographer arrives, the girl tells him about the poltergeist activity and that it never happens when anyone is watching. Therefore, she suggests, he should set up the camera on the tripod but look away when she calls out to snap the picture. And so it happens as she instructs—except that the photographer peeks and catches her in the act of lifting the receiver and throwing it past her; she is caught in the act of fraud.

Why did she engage in this dishonest behavior? What could she possibly gain? In the course of interviewing her, it became clear that she sought attention and even dreamed of a movie being made of her story. The reasons for fraud are many; the perpetrator hopes to sell the story for a book, TV special, or movie, or increase the real estate value of the home assuming that a haunted house would bring more money on the market, or get the attention from family, friends, or loved ones that was sorely missed and very much needed, or act out this drama as a cry for help, hoping on perhaps an unconscious level to be caught and finally receive the psychological help desperately needed to relieve deep-seated emotional problems. The point is that the discovery that some specific poltergeist activity is an act of fraud may only mark the beginning of lengthy analysis and treatment.

In a second case, where a teenager reports to us that she is experiencing poltergeist activity at home, we are obligated to explore and hopefully rule out the hypothesis of fraud. In order to rule out conscious fraud, the teenager should first be interviewed by professionals, then agree to take a polygraph (lie detector) test, administered by a trained interpreter, and subsequently be examined by a certified psychologist. Finally, all of the professionals involved must agree that there was no conscious act of fraud. Even if we have demonstrated that there was no conscious fraud committed, we have not established that the phenomena reported are objectively real and have actually taken place. All that we have established is that she sincerely believes that she has seen poltergeist phenomena. In order to establish the existence of an activity, careful observation must take place by trained scientists who, after filming, video-taping, and recording the events, can rule out both consciously and unconsciously committed acts of fraud.

Unconscious acts of fraud do occur when the agent enters a dissociative state, disconnected from the outside world and, in a trance-like, self-induced hypnotic state acts out on objects around her or him while believing that an external entity or mischievous ghost is causing the poltergeist activity.

Fraud has often been committed by a wide range of people of different ages who, using simple stage magic and prestidigitation (sleight-of-hand), have even fooled professional scientists. The arch-skeptic, professional magician, and leading debunker in the field of psychic phenomena is James Randi, also known by his stage name, "The Amazing Randi." Randi was convinced that even scientists can be fooled, so he enlisted the aid of several teenagers who were adept at stage magic. He had them visit a number of parapsychology laboratories to see if they could convince the scientists who tested them that they possessed psychic talents such as ESP and PK. In this experiment, which Randi called Project Alpha, the teenaged magicians did so well on psychic tests that the parapsychologists published their findings depicting these boys as genuine psychics. Upon publication of this research, Randi went to the media proclaiming that fraud was easily perpetrated on conventional scientists, thereby casting doubt on all of their previous research. He then offered to train scientists on the use of magic and trickery in the parapsychology laboratory so that future research would have greater scientific respectability. With this training, parapsychologists would be better equipped to evaluate demonstrations of the paranormal.

The Psychological and Naturalistic Hypothesis

After both conscious and unconscious fraud have been ruled out and the sincerity of our teenaged witness has been established, we need to further determine the objective reality of the events. In a number of cases, poltergeists have been proven to be nothing more than illusions, or cases of mistaken identity.

Illusions represent mistakes made by the observer in identifying what is seen. In one case, the strange, ghostly figures observed by the witness and only by this witness turned out to be a misrepresentation of the tiny fibrils, or "floaters," that glide by the retina within the vitreous humor of the eye sac. When you look about, these floaters in the liquid of your own eye can be mistaken for ghosts floating about in the outside world.

Another example of an illusion is typical of the kind of mistake that can be made in dimly lit or darkened places. In this case, the witness opened the door of her darkened, unlit room, saw what appeared to be a head in the window silhouetted by the bright, moonlit sky, and screamed. Family members came running to see her pointing at the evil-looking, ghostly head in the window. After someone flicked on the lights, much to the family's amusement but to the witness' embarrassment, the head turned out to be the large geranium blossom growing out of the flower pot on the window sill.

Hallucinations constitute another class of sightings and these are not simply misperceptions of real objects (such as geranium plants). Hallucinations, which are sightings of things that are not out there in the real world, can be caused by psychological disorders, unexpressed or repressed psychological needs, internal biochemical imbalance, drugs (including hallucinogens such as LSD), and even by suggestion.

Suggestion and its power was entertainingly demonstrated one night in Canada by the Amazing Kreskin, the world-famous illusionist. Kreskin brought five adults outdoors into a grassy field on a particularly clear, starlit night, far from the street lights of the city. Assuring the television audience that he had not hypnotized these subjects, he proceeded to direct their attention to a very bright star above them, and the five easily located it.

"How peculiar," Kreskin remarked, "that the star is beginning to pulsate and move ever so slightly, back and forth."

"Yes," all five agreed; they could see its slight but erratic movements, even though no one in the viewing audience could.

"Now," Kreskin observed in a louder, more firm, convincing voice, "look at the strange way it is moving, making right-angle turns as no earthly airplane could."

"Yes," they agreed. They could all see it exactly as he was describing it.

And so, Kreskin concluded, the power of suggestion is very great indeed, for nothing was moving in that night sky as those of us watching the television screen could plainly see. The lesson here is that if the psychological motivation is great, anyone can be talked into seeing anything. Suggestion can create a "mass hysteria" where, in the absence of any real occurrence, a group of people can be made to see all kinds of strange phenomena and later swear to it. A number of innocent people accused of witchcraft may have been the victims of such mass hysteria, and the last words they heard may have been, "burn witch, burn."

Self-hypnosis can be used for many beneficial purposes. For example, you can learn to put yourself into a trance state to reduce brain activity, become relaxed, clear your mind of distracting thoughts, dissociate from the world external to you, and focus all of your attention inward, *thereby rendering yourself highly suggestible*. In this state, you can either *receive* suggestions from audio-tapes (such as those that suggest you quit smoking, or stop overeating, or relax in order to lower blood pressure and eliminate migraine headaches), or *give yourself* suggestions. In this dream-like state, you may give yourself any of a range of suggestions, including the suggestion that you can read minds telepathically, see things happening at a distance clairvoyantly, look into the future using your talent of precognition, or see events that happened in the past through your retrocognitive talent. In addition to suggesting or programming yourself to use and develop your ESP talents, you may also suggest the release of your psychokinetic energy in order to move, break, or levitate objects. Finally, you may try to contact spirits such as departed relatives and loved ones, or even persons who played significant roles in the history of humanity.

Parapsychologists have experimented with hypnosis because it has shown promise in the development of psychic talents. The hypnotic state is one in which there is a dramatic reduction in the distractions of the outside world and an increased ability to focus attention on the suggestion of the moment. However, there are limitations; contrary to myth, the hypnotized person is usually awake and aware throughout the trance state and has the power to snap out of the trance whenever it becomes desirable to do so. (The caution given is that some people are so disturbed and emotionally unstable that, whether in a hypnotized state or not, their behavior is unpredictable and potentially destructive to themselves or to others around them.)

In such a state of suggestibility and dream-like trance, you may begin to imagine that strange things are happening, such as ghosts, levitating or disappearing objects, and an array of poltergeist activity. On the other hand, you may, in trance, be releasing your PK energy and, without realizing it, become the unconscious agent causing things to go bump and crash in the night. To you, this poltergeist activity may appear to be the mischief of an otherworld entity.

In very impressive demonstrations, hypnotists have shown what can be done with suggestion. For example, one hypnotized subject was told that the piece of chalk he was looking at was a lit cigarette, and when it was placed on the skin of his forearm, a blister appeared. People who suffer from the neurotic condition of hysteria will at times bleed from the skin, show the stigmata, reveal bite marks, or have welts that appear and disappear similar to the physical effects that can be produced in a good subject who is in a deep hypnotic trance.

Dreams represent another realm of mind activity that can be mistaken for the real thing and cause you to believe you saw things that were not there. First, vivid dreams need to be ruled out before we conclude that, in fact, you have seen a ghost. Consider the following case:

Mary awakens in the middle of the night convinced that she has seen the spirit of her father, who entered her dream that very night. She is convinced because his appearance is so vivid and real. In addition, she was able to speak with her father while being aware that she was dreaming.

The fact that Mary knew that she was dreaming while experiencing the presence of her father reveals this to have been a *Lucid Dream*. Increasingly, psychologists and parapsychologists are showing people how to make use of a lucid dream in order to help them take control of the dream's direction. For example, psychologists have helped individuals to take control of nightmares through simple suggestion or hypnosis in order to turn nightmares into gentler forms of dreams, or create beneficial, wish-fulfillment dreams. In other instances, parapsychologists have used suggestion to influence the dreamer to use ESP talents in the lucid dream. In lucid dreaming, the dreamer knows that he is dreaming, can therefore take control in the lucid dream and, for example, use his precognitive talent to see his future, the future of loved ones, or the future of some part of the world, galaxy, or universe. The lucid dream presents a unique opportunity to help you take control of your dreams, your talents, your future, your life.

Hypnogogic Images appear just before you fall asleep (in a brain state called theta). These images may arise out of your imagination and, because they appear to be real, may cause you to believe that you have witnessed bizarre poltergeist phenomena. Recent investigations by parapsychologists have demonstrated that, while many hypnogogic images are the work of the imagination revealing the content of your own unconscious mind, other images have proven to be genuinely paranormal. Reports include hearing voices (which later proved to be the thoughts of others), seeing and hearing events taking place many miles away (which later are proven to have occurred), and seeing future events (which later actually do come to pass). The point is that before you fall asleep, hypnogogic images may in fact have paranormal content; you may in fact have seen the ghost behind the poltergeist activity.

Confabulation is one of the most common of naturalistic and psychological explanations for recalling poltergeist or paranormal phenomena that had never actually occurred. Confabulation is a trick that your memory plays on you when you mix together things that you read about, movies and videos you have seen, stories you were told, dreams you had, and fantasies you experienced. Put them all together, mix well, and you may end up with a "false memory" of a poltergeist, UFO, or child abuse.

Recurrent Spontaneous Psychokinesis

RSPK is an alternative parapsychological explanation for poltergeist phenomena that takes us far afield from "fraud" and "naturalistic and psychological explanations"; instead, it takes us deeply into the world of the paranormal. To accept RSPK as a cause of some poltergeists is to accept the reality of psychokinesis as a force that emanates from the living. We believe that the evidence described in our chapter, "The Poltergeist in the Laboratory," clearly establishes the reality of psychokinesis, or PK. It is most probable that to be human is to have the potential to manifest PK. While we presented cases of individuals who were able to use their PK consciously by an act of will, many reported cases of ghosts or poltergeists seem to be caused by the unconscious processes of the agent's mind. In a previous chapter, you read of several individuals whose PK energy left their bodies without their awareness as an expression of their pent-up, repressed sexual drives. We then saw how the release of this energy randomly acted on material objects. Finally, we concluded that, while these unconscious agents believed that they were being harassed by demons or mischievous ghosts, the reality was that they, themselves, had caused and created the poltergeist onslaught.

Survival Phenomena

After thorough investigation, and having ruled out the hypotheses of fraud, naturalistic and psychological causes, ESP and PK, we are left with the survival, or theta, hypothesis. For many scientists and working parapsychologists, this poses the greatest challenge, because the survival hypothesis is based on the premise that the human personality or spirit survives the death of the body. Some scientists refer to this as the theta hypothesis, the letter theta being the first letter of the Greek work for death, thanatos.

In Chapter 4, you will recall reading Hans Holzer's theory that, if a person dies suddenly and unexpectedly, as in a car accident or as a murder victim, the ghost remains in the place in which it died, frightened, confused, angry, disoriented, without a clear sense of what has happened and without the clear knowledge that the body has died. In such a state, the ghost does not enter into the next dimension of existence but, rather, seeks to contact the living by any and every means. These entities will break or throw objects, open and close doors, and even bite, kick, and scratch some person or family member in order to get the attention and help they require. According to this theory, if the death is expected, is slow in coming, or "timely," the spirit leaves the living to be guided into the next dimension of existence by loved ones or significant others from one's own past life. In such cases, the living go on to fulfill their lives in this world, and the spirits of the departed continue the adventure in some other realm.

Chaos Theory, originating in meteorology and the study of weather phenomena, does give us some insights into the theory of poltergeists as suggested to us by the psychic, Donna

D'Alessandro. According to chaos theory, a small amount of energy, such as the flapping of a butterfly's wings, can influence a weather system that is in delicate balance, producing ever increasing wind and air turbulence until a hurricane is created. Donna's view is that the energy of some ghosts and spirits is simply not strong enough to produce all the poltergeist activity witnessed. If even a very small amount of PK energy from the living person is added to that of the ghost, then large material objects can be affected. The tiny amount of PK energy provided by the living agent may contribute to the ghost's energy to set off a cyclone of poltergeist activity. In discussing Donna's hypothesis, it occurred to us that the model that chaos theory provides is a perfect fit with some poltergeist activity observed. While this may be the first attempt to use the chaos theory paradigm to explain some poltergeist phenomena, we suspect that, in the future, other features of this theory will yield additional fruit.

The search continues for the origin and nature of poltergeists by scientists who are truly committed to *scientia,* the search for truth no matter where it leads. If, at the end of the search, ghosts and spirits and poltergeists and all of the causes and hypotheses we have described prove to be true, we should not be frightened or put off, for what we will have revealed is a world far richer and more diverse than ever could have been imagined, had we not engaged in the great adventure of pursuing truth in every corner of the universe.

Bibliography

Adare, Lord. *Experiences in Spiritualism with Mr. D. D. Home.* Originally published in London, 1869. Reprinted by Ayer Co., 1976.

Barry, J. "Retarding Fungus Growth by PK." In J. B. Rhine (Ed.), *Progress in Parapsychology.* North Carolina: Seeman Printery Division of Fisher-Harrison Corp., 1973.

Bayless, Raymond. *The Enigma of the Poltergeist.* West Nyack, NY: Parker Publishing Company, 1967.

Bell, Robert. "Stranger than Fiction." *Cornhill Magazine,* 1860.

Bender, Hans. "An Investigation, of Poltergeist Occurences." *Proceedings of the Parapsychological Association,* No. 5, 1968, pp. 31–33.

Berger, Arthur S. and Joyce Berger. *The Encyclopedia of Parapsychology and Psychical Research*. New York: Paragon House, 1991.

Boling, Rick. "Electric Housewife." *Omni,* 11, Nov. 1988, p. 84.

Brabant, Eva, et al (Editors). *The Correspondence of Sigmund Freud and Sandor Ferenczi*, Vol. 1, 1908–1914. Cambridge, MA: The Belknap Press/Harvard University Press, 1994.

Bracker, M. "Mystery in L.I. house deepens; family, experts, police stumped." *The New York Times*, Mar. 4, 1958, pp. 31, 34.

_____. "House of Flying Objects." *The New York Times*, Oct. 30, 1958, p. 63.

_____. "L.I. 'Poltergeist' Stumps Duke Men." *The New York Times*, Aug. 10, 1958, p. 68.

_____. "Professor Seeks L.I. Mystery." *The New York Times,* Feb. 27, 1958, p. 29. (Note: the professor was Dr. J. Gaither Pratt, then assistant director of the Parapsychology Laboratory of Duke University.)

Brier, R. "PK Effect on Plant-Polygraph System." In J. B. Rhine (Ed.), *Progress in Parapsychology*. Durham, NC: Seeman Printery Division of Fisher-Harrison Corp., 1973.

Carrington, Hereward. *Eusapia Palladino and Her Phenomena*. New York: B. W. Dodge & Co., 1909.

_____. *The American Seances with Eusapia Palladino*. New York: Garrett Publications, 1954.

Cavendish, R. (Ed.) *Man, Myth and Magic*. New York: Marshall, 1983.

Cicero. "Argument against taking dreams seriously." In *The World of Dreams*. R. L. Woods, Ed. New York: Random House, 1947.

Cox, W. E. "PK on pendulum system." In J. B. Rhine (Ed.), *Progress in Parapsychology*. North Carolina: Seeman Printery Division of Fisher-Harrison Corp., 1973.

Crookes, William. "Experimental Investigation of a New Force." *Quarterly Journal of Science,* July 1, 1871.

Crowe, Catherine. *The Night Side of Nature*. Philadelphia: Henry T. Coates & Co., 1901 (originally published in 1848).

Darwin, Charles. *The origin of species by means of natural selection.* Cambridge, MA: Harvard University Press, 1964 (originally published in London by John Murray, 1859).

Feather, S. R. and Rhine, J. B. "A Help-Hinder Comparison." In J. B. Rhine (Ed.), *Progress in Parapsychology*. Durham, NC: Seeman Printery Division of Fisher-Harrison Corp., 1973.

Fishman, S. "Questions for the Cosmos." *The New York Times Magazine*, November 26, 1989.

Flaceliere, R. *Greek Oracles*. Translated by Douglas Garman. London: Elek Books, 1965.

Flammarion, Camille. *Haunted Houses*. London: T. Fisher Unwin, Ltd., 1924.

Fodor, Nandor. *Encyclopaedia of Psychic Science*. Seacaucus, NJ: The Citadel Press, 1974.

_____. *Freud, Jung, and Occultism*. University Books, Inc., 1971.

_____. *On the Trail of the Poltergeist*. New York: The Citadel Press, 1959.

_____. "The Poltergeist—Psychoanalyzed." *Psychiatric Quarterly*, 22, 1948, p. 198.

Fort, Charles. *Book of the Damned*, reprinted in *The Complete Works of Charles Fort*. New York: Dover, 1975.

Gaddis, V. *Mysterious Lights and Fires*.

Gauld, Alan and Cornell, A. D. *Poltergeists*. London: Routledge & Kegan Paul, 1979.

Herodotus. *The History of Herodotus*. Translated by George Rawlinson. New York: Dial Press, 1928.

Home, Daniel Dunglas. *Incidents of My Life, Series One*. London: 1863.

Home, Daniel Dunglas. *Lights and Shadows of Spiritualism*. London: Virtue & Co., 1877.

Home, Mrs. D. D. *D. D. Home: His Life and Mission*. New York: Ayer Publishing, 1976. (This biography by Home's second wife was originally published in London by Trubner & Co., 1888.)

Hurwood, B. J. *Passport to the Supernatural*. New York: Taplinger, 1972.

Inglis, Brian. *Natural and Supernatural: A History of the Paranormal*, Revised edition. Garden City Park, NY: Avery Publishing Group, 1992.

Irwin, H. J. *An Introduction to Parapsychology*. Jefferson, NV: McFarland and Co., Inc., 1989.

Jenkins, Elizabeth. *The Shadow and the Light: A Defense of Daniel Dunglas Home, the Medium*. London: Hamish Hamilton, 1982.

Kardec, Allan. *The Spirit's Book*. Lake Livravia, São Paulo: Editora Ltda, 1856.

Karger, F. and Zicha, G. "Physical investigation of psychokinetic phenomena in Rosenheim, Germany, 1967." *Proceedings of the Parapsychological Association*, No. 5, 1968, pp. 33–35.

Karlsen, Carol F. *The Devil in the Shape of a Woman*. NewYork: W. W. Norton & Company, 1984.

Kerner, Justinus. *The Seeress of Prevorst*. London: J. C. Moore, 1845 (originally published in Stuttgart, 1829).

Lang, Andrew. *Cock Lane and Common Sense*. London: Longmans, Green and Co., 1894.

Leslie, Shane. *Ghost Book*. London: Hollis & Carter, 1955.

Lombroso, Cesare. *After Death, What?* London: T. Fisher Unwin, 1909. Reprinted New York: Harper Row, 1988.

_____. *Criminal Man.* New York: Putnam's Sons, 1911

McCabe, Joseph. *Spiritualism.* London: T. Fisher Unwin, Ltd., 1920. New York: Dodd, Mead & Co.

Ostrander, Sheila. *Psychic Discoveries Behind the Iron Curtain.* New York: Bantam, 1970.

Ostrander, Sheila and Lynn Schroeder. *Handbook of Psi Discoveries.* New York: Berkeley Publishing Co., 1974.

Owen, A. R. G. *Can We Explain the Poltergeist?* New York: Garett Publications, 1964.

Owen, I. M. and M. Sparrow. *Conjuring Up Philip: An Adventure in Psychokinesis.* New York: Harper and Row, 1976.

Podmore, Frank. *Modern Spiritualism: A History and a Criticism.* Vol II. London: Methuen, 1902.

Pratt, J. G. and W. G. Roll. "The Seaford Disturbances." *The Journal of Parapsychology*, No. 22, June 1958, pp. 79–123.

Price, Harry. *Poltergeist: Tales of the Supernatural.* London: Bracken Books, 1993.

_____. Report in *Proceedings of the National Laboratory of Psychical Research,* 1927.

Rawcliffe, D. H. *Occult & Supernatural Phenomena.* New York: Dover Publications, 1989.

Robbins, Russell. The Encyclopedia of Witchcraft and Demonology. London: Spring Books, 1950.

Robinson, Diana M. *To Stretch a Plank: A Survey of Psychokinesis.* Chicago: Nelson-Hall, 1981.

Rogo, D. Scott. *Minds and Motion: The Riddle of Psychokinesis.* New York: Taplingen Publishing Co., 1978.

_____. *On the Track of the Poltergeist.* Englewood Cliffs, NJ: Prentice-Hall, 1986.

Roll, William G. *The Poltergeist.* Garden City, NY: Nelson Doubleday, 1972.

Saggs, H. W. F. *The Greatness that was Babylon.*

Smith, Eleanor. *Psychic People.* New York: William Morrow & Co., 1968.

Starbird, Ethel A. "New York's Land of Dreamers and Doers." *National Geographic*, Vol. 151, No. 5, May 1977, pp. 702–724.

Steinour, Harold. *Exploring the Unseen World.* New York: The Citadel Press, 1959.

Thurston, Herbert. *Ghosts and Poltergeists.* London: Burns Oates & Washbourne, 1953.

Ullman, Montague & Krippner, Stanley. *Dream Telepathy: Experiments in Nocturnal ESP.* New York: Macmillan, 1973.

Van Over, Raymond. *Psychology and Extrasensory Perception.* New York: The New American Library, Inc., 1972.

Vann, L., Ed. *The FRNM Bulletin.* Durham, NC: Parapsychology Press of the Foundation for Research on the Nature of Man, No. 39, 1988, p. 2.

Wilson, Colin. *The Mammoth Book of the Supernatural.* New York: Carroll & Graf Publishers, 1991.

Index

Stay in Touch. . .

Llewellyn publishes hundreds of books on your favorite subjects

On the following pages you will find listed some books now available on related subjects. Your local bookstore stocks most of these and will stock new Llewellyn titles as they become available. We urge your patronage.

Order by Phone

Call toll-free within the U.S. and Canada, **1–800–THE MOON**.
In Minnesota call **(612) 291–1970**.
We accept Visa, MasterCard, and American Express.

Order by Mail

Send the full price of your order (MN residents add 7% sales tax) in U.S. funds to:

Llewellyn Worldwide
P.O. Box 64383, Dept. K682–3
St. Paul, MN 55164–0383, U.S.A.

Postage and Handling

- $4.00 for orders $15.00 and under
- $5.00 for orders over $15.00
- No charge for orders over $100.00

We ship UPS in the continental United States. We cannot ship to P.O. boxes. Orders shipped to Alaska, Hawaii, Canada, Mexico, and Puerto Rico will be sent first-class mail.

International orders: Airmail—add freight equal to price of each book to the total price of order, plus $5.00 for each non-book item (audiotapes, etc.). Surface mail—Add $1.00 per item.

Allow 4–6 weeks delivery on all orders. Postage and handling rates subject to change.

Group Discounts

We offer a 20% quantity discount to group leaders or agents. You must order a minimum of 5 copies of the same book to get our special quantity price.

Free Catalog

Get a free copy of our color catalog, *New Worlds of Mind and Spirit*. Subscribe for just $10.00 in the United States and Canada ($20.00 overseas, first class mail). Many bookstores carry *New Worlds*—ask for it!

DOORS TO OTHER WORLDS
A Practical Guide to Communicating
with Spirits

Raymond Buckland

There has been a revival of spiritualism in recent years, with more and more people attempting to communicate with disembodied spirits via talking boards, séances, and all forms of mediumship (e.g., allowing another spirit to make use of your vocal chords, hand muscles, etc., while you remain in control of your body). The movement, which began in 1848 with the Fox sisters of New York, has attracted the likes of Abraham Lincoln and Queen Victoria, and even blossomed into a full-scale religion with regular services of hymns, prayers, Bible-reading and sermons along with spirit communication.

Doors to Other Worlds is for *anyone* who wishes to communicate with spirits, as well as for the less adventurous who simply wish to satisfy their curiosity about the subject. Explore the nature of the Spiritual Body, learn how to prepare yourself to become a medium, experience for yourself the trance state, clairvoyance, psychometry, table tipping and levitation, talking boards, automatic writing, spiritual photography, spiritual healing, distant healing, channeling, development circles, and also learn how to avoid spiritual fraud.
0–87542–061–3, 272 pp., 5 ¼ x 8, illus., softcover   **$10.00**

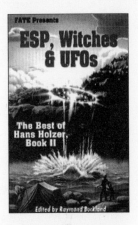

ESP, WITCHES & UFOS:
The Best of Hans Holzer, Book II

Edited by Raymond Buckland

In this exciting anthology, best-selling author and psychic investigator Hans Holzer explores true accounts of the strange and unknown: telepathy, psychic and reincarnation dreams, survival after death, psycho-ecstasy, unorthodox healings, Pagans and Witches, and Ufonauts. Reports included in this volume:

- Mrs. F. dreamed of a group of killers and was particularly frightened by the eyes of their leader. Ten days later, the Sharon Tate murders broke into the headlines. When Mrs. F. saw the photo of Charles Manson, she immediately recognized him as the man from her dream
- How you can use four simple "wish-fulfillment" steps to achieve psycho-ecstasy—turning a negative situation into something positive
- Several true accounts of miraculous healings achieved by unorthodox medical practitioners
- How the author, when late to meet with a friend and unable to find a telephone nearby, sent a telepathic message to his friend via his friend's answering service
- The reasons why more and more people are turning to Witchcraft and Paganism as a way of life
- When UFOs land: physical evidence vs. cultists

These reports and many more will entertain and enlighten all readers intrigued by the mysteries of life … and beyond!

0–87542–368–X, 304 pp., mass market   **$4.95**

GHOSTS, HAUNTINGS &
POSSESSIONS
The Best of Hans Holzer, Book I

Edited by Raymond Buckland

Now, a collection of the best stories from best-selling author and
psychic investigator Hans Holzer—in mass market format! Accounts
in *Ghosts, Hauntings & Possessions* include:

- A 37-year-old housewife from Nebraska was tormented by a ghost
  that drove phantom cars and grabbed her foot while she lay in bed
  at night. Even after moving to a different state, she could still hear
  heavy breathing.
- Here is the exact transcript of what transpired in a seance con-
  frontation with Elvis Presley—almost a year after his death!
- Ordinary people from all over the country had premonitions about
  the murders of John and Robert Kennedy. Here are their stories.
- What happened to the middle-aged woman who played with the
  Ouija board and ended up tormented and possessed by the spirit of
  a former boyfriend?
- Here is the report of Abraham Lincoln's prophetic dream of his
  own funeral. Does his ghost still roam the White House because of
  unfinished business?

These stories and many more will intrigue, spook and entertain readers of all ages.

0–87542–367–1, 288 pp., mass market **$5.99**

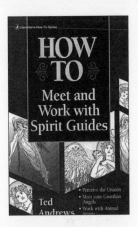

HOW TO MEET & WORK WITH SPIRIT GUIDES

Ted Andrews

We often experience spirit contact in our lives but fail to recognize it for what it is. Now you can learn to access and attune to beings such as guardian angels, nature spirits and elementals, spirit totems, archangels, gods and goddesses—as well as family and friends after their physical death.

Contact with higher soul energies strengthens the will and enlightens the mind. Through a series of simple exercises, you can safely and gradually increase your awareness of spirits and your ability to identify them. You will learn to develop an intentional and directed contact with any number of spirit beings. Discover meditations to open up your subconscious. Learn which acupressure points effectively stimulate your intuitive faculties. Find out how to form a group for spirit work, use crystal balls, perform automatic writing, attune your aura for spirit contact, use sigils to contact the great archangels and much more! Read *How to Meet and Work with Spirit Guides* and take your first steps through the corridors of life beyond the physical.

0–87542–008–7, 192 pp., mass market, illus.   **$4.99**

HOW TO UNCOVER YOUR PAST LIVES

by Ted Andrews

Knowledge of your past lives can be extremely rewarding. It can assist you in opening to new depths within your own psychological makeup. It can provide greater insight into present circumstances with loved ones, career and health. It is also a lot of fun.

Now Ted Andrews shares with you nine different techniques that you can use to access your past lives. Between techniques, Andrews discusses issues such as karma and how it is expressed in your present life; the source of past life information; soul mates and twin souls; proving past lives; the mysteries of birth and death; animals and reincarnation; abortion and pre-mature death; and the role of reincarnation in Christianity.

To explore your past lives, you need only use one or more of the techniques offered. Complete instructions are provided for a safe and easy regression. Learn to dowse to pinpoint the years and places of your lives with great accuracy, make your own self-hypnosis tape, attune to the incoming child during pregnancy, use the tarot and the cabala in past life meditations, keep a past life journal and more.
0–87542–022–2, 240 pp., mass market, illus.   **$4.99**

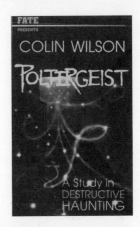

POLTERGEIST
A Study in Destructive Haunting

Colin Wilson

Objects flying through the air, furniture waltzing around the room, dishes crashing to the floor. These are the hallmarks of the poltergeist phenomena. Now Colin Wilson, the renowned authority on the paranormal, investigates these mysterious forces in this fascinating and provocative work.

A middle-aged businessman and his wife rented a house on Cape Cod for the summer. They were, for some reason, its first occupants in nine years. Neither paid much attention to the first disturbance—a tapping near the front door. But then they heard a clicking noise—followed by a deafening crash from the garage . . . What happened next is revealed only in *Poltergeist!*

Countless similar cases of poltergeist mischief have been recorded from the days of ancient Greece and Rome to the present. But what are poltergeists? Where do they come from? Why do they appear and how do they interact in our world? In this comprehensive study, Colin Wilson examines the evidence regarding poltergeists and develops a masterful and definitive theory of the forces that surround us and are contained within each one of us.

0–87542–883–5, 448 pp., mass market   **$5.95**

SUMMONING SPIRITS
The Art of Magical Evocation

Konstantinos

Evoking spirits is one of the most powerful and beneficial magical techniques you can use. But for centuries, this technique has either been kept secret or revealed in unusable fragments by those with little practical evocation experience. *Summoning Spirits* is a complete training manual, written by a practicing magician. This book makes performing evocations easy to do, even if you've never performed a magical ritual before.

Using the simple instructions in this manual, you can summon spiritual entities to effect miraculous changes in your life. Obtain mystical abilities ... locate hidden "treasure" ... control the weather ... even command a spirit "army" to protect your home while you're away! Each entity has its own special expertise—this book names and describes entities you can evoke to help you succeed in various tasks. You will learn how to perform evocations to both the astral and physical planes, plus opening and banishing rituals. Do exercises designed to prepare you for magical workings and astral travel, discover how to create a manufactured spirit, consecrate your magical implements and much more. Includes complete sample rituals.
1–56718–381–6, 240 pp., 7 x 10, softcover   **$14.95**

TRUE HAUNTINGS
Spirits With a Purpose

Hazel M. Denning, Ph.D.

Do spirits feel and think? Does death automatically promote them to a paradise—or as some believe, a hell? Real-life ghostbuster Dr. Hazel M. Denning reveals the answers through case histories of the friendly and hostile earthbound spirits she has encountered. Learn the reasons spirits remain entrapped in the vibrational force field of the earth: fear of going to the other side, desire to protect surviving loved ones, and revenge. Dr. Denning also shares fascinating case histories involving spirit possession, psychic attack, mediumship and spirit guides. Find out why spirits haunt us in True Hauntings, the only book of its kind written from the perspective of the spirits themselves.

1–56718–218–6, 240 pp., 6 x 9, index, glossary, softbound $12.95

PSYCHIC EMPOWERMENT
A 7-Day Plan for Self-Development

Joe Slate, Ph.D.

Use 100% of your mind power in just one week! You've heard it before: each of us is filled with an abundance of untapped power—yet we only use *one-tenth* of its potential. Now a clinical psychologist and famed researcher in parapsychology shows you *how* to probe your mind's psychic faculties and manifest your capacity to *access* the higher planes of the mind.

The psychic experience validates your true nature and connects you to your inner knowing. Dr. Slate reveals the life-changing nature of psychic phenomena—including telepathy, out-of-body experiences and automatic writing. At the same time, he shows you how to develop a host of psychic abilities including psychokinesis, crystal gazing, and table tilting.

The final section of the book outlines his accelerated 7-Day Psychic Development Plan through which you can unleash your innate power and wisdom without further delay.

ISBN: 1-56718-635-1, 6 x 9, 256 pp., softbound   **$12.95**

PSYCHIC PETS & SPIRIT ANIMALS
True Stories from the Files of FATE Magazine

FATE Magazine Editorial Staff

In spite of all our scientific knowledge about animals, important questions remain about the nature of animal intelligence. Now, a large body of personal testimony compels us to raise still deeper questions. Are some animals, like some people, psychic? If human beings survive death, do animals? Do bonds exist between people and animals that are beyond our ability to comprehend?

Psychic Pets & Spirit Animals is a varied collection from the past 50 years of the real-life experiences of ordinary people with creatures great and small. You will encounter psychic pets, ghost animals, animal omens, extraordinary human-animal bonds, pet survival after death, phantom protectors and the weird creatures of cryptozoology. Dogs, cats, birds, horses, wolves, grizzly bears—even insects—are the heroes of shockingly true reports that illustrate just how little we know about the animals we think we know best.

The true stories in *Psychic Pets & Spirit Animals* suggest that animals are, in many ways, more like us than we think—and that they, too, can step into the strange and unknowable realm of the paranormal, where all things are possible.

1–56718–299–2, 272 pp., mass market, softcover   **$4.99**

**PSYCHIC DEVELOPMENT
FOR BEGINNERS**
An Easy Guide to Releasing and
Developing Your Psychic Abilities

William Hewitt

Psychic Development for Beginners provides detailed instruction on developing your sixth sense, or psychic ability. Improve your sense of worth, your sense of responsibility and therefore your ability to make a difference in the world. Innovative exercises like "The Skyscraper" allow beginning students of psychic development to quickly realize personal and material gain through their own natural talent.

Benefits range from the practical to spiritual. Find a parking space anywhere, handle a difficult salesperson, choose a compatible partner, and even access different time periods! Practice psychic healing on pets or humans—and be pleasantly surprised by your results. Use psychic commands to prevent dozing while driving. Preview out-of-body travel, cosmic consciousness and other alternative realities. Instruction in *Psychic Development for Beginners* is supported by personal anecdotes, 44 psychic development exercises, and 28 related psychic case studies to help students gain a comprehensive understanding of the psychic realm.
1-56718-360-3, 5¼ x 8, 216 pp., softcover
$9.95